CHANGES

Presented to

CHANGES

One Family's Journey with a Transgender Teen

Susan Butler

Chandler Palladino

Ashlea Palladino

Acknowledgments

I have learned many lessons from my children over the years, but none quite so poignant as striving to understand and appreciate the challenges of a transgender child, a concept until now quite foreign to me. As you will learn in this book, my family has been through tremendous struggles, broken hearts, and ongoing restoration.

Chandler, our beloved grandson, is the reason for writing *Changes.* When I asked him if he would like to collaborate in the writing, he jumped at the chance to be heard in order to gain understanding for himself and all the transitioning teens in the world. As you will learn, he is gifted in communicating through the written word, speech and song. We are proud of his accomplishments, but mostly, we are in love with Chandler's heart and soul.

Ashlea, our daughter, is not only Chandler's mother, but the third collaborator in our triangulated tale. She is accomplished at whatever task she sets out to do, and has been vital in giving a third viewpoint with candor and beautiful expression. She helped me balance and soften our story, always keeping in mind the reading audience. Her undergraduate degree in English makes her the perfect editor, for which I am confidently grateful. She also edited my first book, *First Fruits,* published in 2016. Ashlea has now begun her Master's field of study in Social Justice and Human Rights at SMU. We love and admire our amazing Ashlea.

C.J., my forever husband, is also a man of patience, humor and candor. There have been tense moments in this real-life drama, where C.J. has used these individual traits, usually with good timing! I am thankful he gives me room to spread my wings and do that which I am led to do. His support is appreciated more than he realizes. I am blessed to call C.J. my rock, the man I love and admire.

Finally, I want to thank my family and friends for caring enough to take this journey into the unknown world of transgender life with us. It is at best a challenge for anyone who is not directly affected, and so I will just say, "You know who you are, and I love you deeply for coming alongside us. We will never forget your hearts in supporting us through this."

CHANGES

One Family's Journey with a Transgender Teen

©2019 Susan Butler

ISBN: 9781795448215

DEDICATION
to
OUR FAMILY

FOR THE DETERMINATION AND
STRENGTH TO LOVE AND
UNDERSTAND EACH OTHER.

FOR THE GRACE WE EXTEND
TO EACH OTHER BECAUSE OF THE
GRACE GIVEN TO US.

Contents

LIFE

Life is amazing.

And then it's awful.

And then it's amazing again.

And in between the amazing and awful,

It's ordinary and mundane and routine.

Breathe in the amazing,

Hold on through the awful,

And exhale during the ordinary.

That's just living heartbreaking—soul-healing

Amazing—awful—ordinary life.

And it's breathtakingly beautiful.[1]

---

[1] L. R. Knost. Child development best-selling author. On Facebook and at www.LRKnost.com

Prologue

What would you do if someone you love deeply suddenly announced they were not the person you thought you knew? This is the story of one family's journey into the deep waters of denial, realization, consternation, grief, conflict and acceptance, armed with the Truth of God's Word and a determination to understand.

If you have picked up this book, your interest may be a simple curiosity, or you may be searching for a glimmer of hope in your own unwieldy situation. For those reading this because they want to know more about the transgender personality, we provide information about our personal struggles and scientific discovery. For those in the experience right now, we want to give you some encouragement that your situation is not impossible. We also want to broach some hard questions that those inside and outside the transgender community are asking:

1. Is there a need for better understanding of those whose gender is in question?

2. Is there justification for the transgender individuals who are socially dismissed or met with bullying because of their differences?

3. WWJD—What *would* Jesus Do—to respond to the bombardment of situational ethics questions we encounter?

Let us reason together, and accept that we may not come to the same conclusions on every topic, but that we might have a better understanding of those whose opinions differ from ours. Is it not true that we seek to understand that which affects us most personally? Whether it's a child's learning disorder, a rare form of cancer, the deteriorating memory of a loved one, or as in this case, a beloved family member who is certain that his gender is diametrically opposite of all physical proof to the contrary—we want knowledge and understanding so that we might regain our equilibrium, and above all else, love with a pure heart.

The historical solar eclipse of 2017 happened today, where the moon eclipsed 70% of the sun in the Dallas area. As I stared through my protective lenses, it struck me how well I could see my surroundings with only 30% of the sun's illumination. As we search for knowledge and understanding (as through a glass darkly), we may not be able to see 100%, but we can certainly be enlightened by the Light that is promised to those who seek.

As we tell our story, you will perhaps share in our own discovery that there can be justification for more than one response to an issue. We share several perspectives earnestly, honestly, and unvarnished—believing that this approach will open dialogue between teens, parents and other family members.

5

The Family

Susan Butler

Early Life as Caroline
—BY CHANDLER—

I have always been a boy. My family and my doctors would not agree.

I didn't see what my family saw in me as a toddler—curls, ruby red lips, playing dress-up, and love-in-the-extreme of stuffed "am-i-nals." But, at the same time, my family didn't see what I imagined, looking from the inside out—having strong muscles, winning battles with swords (mostly made with vacuum cleaner tubes), being protected by super frogs ("Shroggies") and Taekwondo at six and seven, where I mastered self-defense by breaking boards with my bare hands!

My doctors saw growth patterns that were at the top of the charts for height and weight. Since my parents and my uncle were also above average, growth plate pain was an inherited trait. Sometimes it was fun being the tallest in my class; other times my teachers expected me to be more mature. That's like thinking the student with the thickest glasses is always the smartest kid in the class.

I have never felt very feminine despite my golden curls. Even as a little kid, from how I dressed to how I acted around my friends and family, I always wanted to lift the heavy groceries or show off my muscles to the girls at school. The summer I turned three, I had a pink ruffled dress that was super soft. I wore it a few times because I liked soft things. But, if Mom ever gave me the option of wearing the pink dress or basketball shorts and a tee, I would choose the shorts and tee. Then again, if she gave me the choice of wearing clothes or wearing nothing, I would choose to be naked. To this day, my favorite thing is to come home from school and lose my shirt. Never once did I openly say, "Please let me wear the pink dress, Mom!" It was always, "Can I get some new sneakers to go with my basketball shorts?"

Now, I understand that some would say I did indeed show all the signs of a "tomboy." To me, I was just another little boy. I remember looking in the mirror and flexing my muscles in my Avengers tee because I thought I looked like a guy—not a girl with guy features. Still, at this point, when I was referred to as "she/her" it never upset me. Being a very happy-go-lucky child, I just wanted to sing and dance and have fun with my friends. My life was pretty carefree, and worrying about labels was not even on my radar. Maybe other people did not see the boy I saw, but how I *felt* was the only thing that mattered to me.

Snapshot of Life at Nine
—BY CAROLINE—

This letter from Caroline to her Great Grandpa for his 88th birthday was written the day before we left for San Antonio where my sister, Bonnie, and husband David live. We had a great birthday celebration together with Dad and Mom and their two great grandchildren, which would later be marked as Dad's last birthday. When I uncovered this letter, I remembered how surprisingly shy Caroline was that day, and how she asked me to read this funny, creative letter to my dad. Well, Caroline's name has changed, but the creative and humorous kid is still alive and well! (SUSAN)

"Today is just another day in the Chez Butler house. Just sittin' while playin' "Dogmitten, where's my Kitten?" while Humbug is watching a very sophisticated video. And last, but certainly the fanciest, Mimi — and the crowd goes crazy, "Woohoo, Yay, Booya!" … allll-righty then!

Moving on to Thursday — pack, pack, pack, and Friday — go, go, go on to San Antonio, 5 hours gone. Bring on the babies, but wait … drum roll please … introducing the new "E & G" — ME! "Booyah to the Hooyah, Caroline's in the house — What-What? WORD!"

OK, let's boogie down to Aunt Bonnie — I love your house! It's so pretty, like you! And you have great taste in music … raise your hand if you've heard the song, "MEAN" by Taylor Swift. Aunt Bonnie insisted I play the song on Mimi's iPad when she was at my house. Now let's hippity-hop down to Uncle David and give him a big round of applause - "Booyah to the Hooyah"! You do such a good impression of Donald Duck, and you taught me how to do this (slap hand/chest). Give it up for Uncle David! Let's not forget the Super Dog, Ricky — "I'm super-cool, I'm super-hot, I'm the dog you like a lot — I'm Super, Super

Ricky, I'm Super, Super Ricky!" Let's give a round of applause for Ricky the Super Dog!

Let's move on to LoLo – oh yeah, break it down, now - "Boom ChikaChika, Boom, Boom, Boom!" Let's hear it for LoLo! Who can forget Carson, the man of the house, and an awesome little cuz. Now let's chacha over to Taryn, the awesome, cool, hip mom – now I know where Carson gets his imagination!

Speakin' of little cuzzes, let's introduce the newest member of the family – Antonio! Can I get a "what-what"? And now introducing the new Daddy in the house, Bart! "Booyah, oh yeah."   Fun facts: Martial arts expert, drummer, and the newest role, DADDY! All the babies say, "yeah, YEAH!" Now on to the most caring and loving Mom to Antonio – wow, put your head phones on 'cause when the babies say "yeah," you'll hear sounds for a week, trust me, it's happened before! Introducing Brady! "Woohoo! Yeah, Booyah to the Hooyah! Word."

Okay, now on to the best painter I know – my Great Grandma, Mema. "Woohoo, Booyah, Word to the Mema!" Now introducing (drum roll, please) the Birthday Boy, Grandpa! Oh yeah, break it down. Best poem writer I know, and he is a GREAT Grandpa!

And that's my story . . .

Happy Birthday, Grandpa!"

Ashlea

Chandler's Mom

—BY SUSAN—

Ashlea is our first born—the self-proclaimed "Eldest and the Greatest."

This term of endearment was later shortened to "The E & G" and mentioned quite often through the years, tongue-in-cheek, (and later penned as the title to a poem written by my late father, which he read at the reception of her marriage to Nick).

Only 18 months after CJ and I endured the painful loss of a full-term baby girl, Ashlea entered our world as a *celebration*. Tears of joy were shed and hope reborn as CJ and I were given this precious gift of life. The E & G, of course, put her own spin on this event in a memoir celebrating our 50th anniversary, and I quote: "A couple of years later, I showed up and the sky turned blue and the flowers bloomed and everything was wonderful!"

Those first years were full of fun watching the endless changes in her personality, and her ability to express herself seemingly beyond her years. There were challenges as we realized we had been blessed with a precocious and independent little thinker. James Dobson wrote a book entitled "The Strong-Willed Child"—we think he modeled it after Ashlea. In first grade, she wanted to help the children who didn't understand. This frustrated her teacher, but the principal soon realized Ashlea was just bored, so they let her skip second grade.

As a pre-teen, Ashlea found her passion in singing, both at school and at church. She loved choir and at 15, she was privileged to sing a solo during the church Christmas Festival to audiences of 4,000 each night. We were so proud of her.

Country music was a genre we all enjoyed, and Ashlea easily learned the lyrics to hits by all the popular artists. She joined me at a party one night where we performed one of The Judd's hits. We also took a road trip to Nashville the next summer for the annual Fan Fair. It was so hot, but that didn't stop us from standing in line for *five hours* to get Wynona Judd's autograph. We also got to record "She's in Love with the Boy" in a sound booth with Trisha Yearwood. Ashlea just knew this was the career for her.

As is so often true with the passage of time, her attention turned to more practical career paths. After getting her BA in English from North Texas State University, she got her first full-time commercial property management position, following in the footsteps of her dad. She was still singing karaoke on the weekends, but it seemed her vocation was set in commercial real estate.

Then, along came Nick Palladino, the man who made Ashlea swoon. They were married in the year 2000. We have laughed about the juxtaposition of their career paths—Nick, a commercial garbage truck driver for Waste Management, and Ashlea, a commercial property manager. It only took a couple of years, though, before they realized they might combine their individual expertise. Nick and Ashlea formed a company called RPS (Reliable Property Services) and began working with property managers of buildings, retail centers, and warehouses.

Nick could do just about anything he set his mind to, and combined with his self-assurance and sense of humor—and Ashlea's administrative skills running the office— the managers who hired them were plenty happy with the services provided by RPS.

About the time they started RPS, Ashlea got pregnant. Trying to juggle the business, a dog, and a baby was quite the challenge. They were in an apartment at the time, but were also trying to gain custody of Nick's two sons, Bryce and Nickalous, who were 10 and 8. The boys were good kids, and we all fell in love with them.

Caroline Jordan Palladino came into the world on June 9, 2003… "and the sky was blue and the flowers were blooming and life was just perfect!" I went to their apartment every day to visit this first beautiful grandchild, helping like all first grandmothers do.

Nick and Ashlea were able to buy their first home when Caroline was only a few months old, just in time for the boys to come live with them. It worked well for about a year, but soon enough, the boys' mom wanted them back. Nick felt he had no choice but to let them return to her. It was very hard on him, because his ex-wife rarely let him see his boys after that.

There were many great days with Nick, Ashlea, and Caroline. We celebrated together, took trips together, but mainly just lived life like there would always be another family gathering, another tomorrow. Nick was so funny, and was always dreaming up something to look forward to for his family. He loved his family and his business, usually in that order.

Then, the fateful day came when we realized our lives would be inexorably changed. Nick's death marked all of us, but none so much as Ashlea. I hope you never have to experience watching grief wash over your child—again and again and again. After a beautiful memorial service, Nick's memory was forever etched in our hearts.

For Ashlea, the scenes from their time together would replay over and over. Not every moment was a good moment, but even so, each memory was a treasure. Nick has been gone since 2007, but these nuggets in the treasure chest of Ashlea's memory have been shared with her child often.

Life after Nick brought changes for Caroline, who was enrolled at Legacy Christian Academy where she finished kindergarten and first grade. It was a great learning environment with a small teacher/student ratio. But due to financial constraints, Caroline then attended public school for the rest of elementary and middle school.

She did not seem to suffer from not having a dad around until middle school. Events like daddy-daughter dances and other situations where parents were invited made Nick's absence more obvious. We noticed an impending sadness, and thought his death must finally be coming home to roost.

Though Nick's death played a part in some of Caroline's mood swings, there were hormonal changes causing tidal waves of emotional surges. We were shocked when Caroline began cutting (a regrettably popular form of self-harm using sharp objects to cut the skin). Ashlea took her to a therapist, but found that all Caroline wanted to do was talk to the therapist about the drama going on at school with her friends.

After months of dealing with her cutting, she finally told her mom she thought she liked girls, not boys. But, near the end of 7th grade on April 2, 2016, Caroline confided to Ashlea that she wanted to *be* a boy, having read some online information on those who recognize themselves to be transgender. Caroline felt like it described her perfectly.

Ashlea knew this was going to stir up a rattlesnakes' nest with CJ and me, so she advised Caroline to keep that information between them. Suffice it to say, Caroline wasn't able to keep the charade going for long. Hence, the day came when I confronted Ashlea about the issue, and she confirmed my suspicions. It was not easy for Ashlea, but she tried to take it all in stride, believing it was just a phase. I, on the other hand, felt deep in my soul that this was a life-changing decision—for all of us.

I will say that Ashlea did adjust more quickly to the concept of her child making this change. For her, it was either climb on board with her child, or possibly lose them forever. For CJ and me, it was more complicated, as I will explain later. Ashlea's persona is normally calm, but conversations about transgender issues could cause a firestorm in all of us. She got so tired of dissecting each moment with such regularity. She understood my need to ask questions, and would muster all available patience to provide answers. Her dream is that one day, her child's gender identity won't be the inevitable topic of conversation.

A Mother's Perspective

—BY ASHLEA—

On April 2, 2016 my 13-year old daughter Caroline sat me down on our back porch in Frisco, Texas and tearfully told me she felt like she was a boy. She was born in the wrong body, she said. She wanted to cut off her hair and be addressed as *Chandler*. She wanted me to use male pronouns, she *needed* me to use them. She wanted to start living her new truth, whatever that meant. As I listened to the raw gush of emotion pouring from her pre-teen mouth, I silently prayed, "God, please let this be a phase. Please just let her be a lesbian."

I'd long suspected Caroline was gay, based on many factors and habits: she had a long-standing, obsessive crush on Anne Hathaway, she made up a boyfriend in 5th grade because she thought that's what I wanted to hear, and from the time she could dress herself, she opted for basketball shorts and tank tops "what showed [her] muscles." Caroline had always been an emotionally mature child, much preferring the company of adults to that of other children. So, while I prayed this was just another thing she wanted to try—like Taekwondo or voice lessons—I knew in my heart that Caroline's spring announcement wasn't angsty childish folly.

As I reflect on that day on the porch, I know I didn't cry. I was panicked for what this new path would mean for our family, specifically for my parents. I remember thinking, "Seriously, Ashlea? You're more concerned with what Mom and Dad will think than how this change will affect your child?" It was ludicrous, but it was true: my parents were not going to handle this well. Christianity is the fiber of our entire family. It is the source of all knowledge and the framework under which all decisions are contemplated and carried out. WWJD is not just a saying stamped on a cheap rubber bracelet in my family—it is a comprehensive, complete worldview.

My conservative parents were antipathetic when it came to the subject of LGBTQ matters—a real sticking point between us for most of my life, so I was prepared for the roadblock Chandler's coming out would erect in the family. I started rejecting my parents' ideologies about "family values" morality in my late teens, but only in the past handful of years have I been able to sever many of the ties to their Christianity that don't fit in my developing worldview. That disconnection has been painful for my family, specifically because my parents feel like they've failed with me— that they've not done their jobs as Christ followers if I reject their all-consuming conviction that only Believers will have eternal life. But interestingly, a single point of scientific data altered the course of their understanding with regard to Chandler's coming out as transgender: the realization that 41% of transgender people attempt suicide at some point in their lifetime. This statistic horrified my parents, it scared them, and it ultimately bolstered them to action.

During a 6-month period of unemployment, Chandler and I moved in with my parents and it was tough. Chandler stayed in his room most of the time to avoid listening to my parents call him *she*, and when we did interact, Chandler was full of rage that boiled just beneath the surface. He had always been incredibly close to my mother, and this chasm between them was almost too much to bear, for all of us. One night, Chandler cried to me in my bedroom about the pain he was experiencing, and the isolation he was feeling. My mom happened into the room and we drew her into the discussion. After a few minutes, she pulled my dad, CJ, in as well, and what resulted was the turning point of our progress toward healing as a family. I'm generally a very passive person, not bent toward dramatics or hysteria. But that night, watching my child struggle in torment, my protective instincts kicked in, and I erupted. I told my parents in no uncertain terms that I wouldn't hesitate to pack up Chandler and everything we own and move. Move to Austin to be nearer my brother in a more LGBTQ-friendly part of my beloved Texas. Move to the Pacific Northwest where Chandler would thrive in an environment more suited to his success. Move anywhere, do anything, change everything if it would help him find peace. It was during the conversation that night that I laid out what would become my mantra every day since: If you are not on Team Chandler, I don't have time for you

My mother's idea for us to write a book together as a family was born out of that Sunday night conversation. Having written a book before, she understood the incomputable cathartic value of creativity, and putting thoughts to paper. Mom also recognized the opportunity to help others who might be waging similar battles in their families. Chandler's desire in this life is to be heard and understood and valued, and I knew his unique perspective and voice could potentially move mountains; he was on board to contribute to the book. As I perceived it, my assignment was to mediate between Mom and Chandler, to collaborate with input from my perspective as a mother, and to edit my co-authors. And CJ…well, CJ would do what CJ does best: offer moral support from a distance and supply my mother with his thoughts so that she could write on his behalf. So off we went on yet another familial journey of trial, error, and understanding.

In discussing our goals and target audiences for the book, Chandler and I discovered Mom's objectives were slightly different than our own. Because portions of the book are based in the Christian's perspective (the portions written by Mom), Chandler and I assumed the book would be targeted to Christians who are weaving their way through a trans issue—Christians who are seeking to truly understand the trans community without judgment. Mom's broader vision, however, was to present a loving God to a community of individuals who are often maligned by organized religion. Upon this realization, we made a few structural and content changes to the book in hopes of reaching both goals. For example, we initially used the acronym LGBTQ anywhere in the book where we meant *trans*. We removed all references to LGBQ for two reasons: 1) many in the LGBQ community don't feel the "T" should be included, since LGBQ speaks to sexual orientation, while "T" refers to gender identity, and 2) inclusion of LGBQ discussions has different/deeper ramifications within the context of Christianity and The Bible.

We anticipated some other potential problems with this book. My mom wrote a Christian devotional book called *First Fruits,* published by Morgan James Faith Division (2016). While this work was well-received and promoted within churches and Christian communities in general, I feared this new work would not be met with the same enthusiasm by people she previously counted on as allies of her work. Further, while we have cited scholarly sources and resources, we are not scholarly writers. We each have individual styles and voices, especially Chandler's writing style which very much reflects his emotional 16-year old self. While his rawness might be viewed with a negative lens in another type of book, it is purposeful and meaningful in this scenario.

And so, we reached an equilibrium as a family. Nothing is perfect, and neither is our family. My mom's mom, Lou, lives with my parents a few months out of each year, and even at 94 years of age, Mema does her utmost to respect Chandler by using his new legal name and the appropriate corresponding pronouns. Believe it or not, gruff and grumpy, Southern-fried CJ has shocked us all. He now calls Chandler *man* and *dude*, and when speaking to me, always refers to Chandler as my *son*. Though my parents and I arrived at our varying levels of understanding at different times, in different ways, we share a common concern: life is going to be tough for Chandler. Our collective job is to sure him up in every possible way so that we can send him out into real life with a toolbox full of professional help and guidance, self-respect, and confidence in the fact that he is a singular, incredibly special human being.

I've never felt burdened by Chandler's transition. For me it's just another parental journey I must undertake to complete the raising of my son—just like getting through Algebra homework, or a broken arm, or staying up too late sewing costumes for his school musical. It's my job. But there is no guidebook for this job, no instruction manual to tell me I've missed a step or to affirm me when I've done something right. My hope is that *Changes* will find itself in the hands of another single mother who really needs that affirmation, and then that mother will recommend it to another, and so on until the transgender journey isn't so painful and scary and taboo.

Nick – Life & Death
Chandler's Dad

—BY ASHLEA—

Nick was a really big guy, both physically and in personality. He spoke loudly and with all sorts of authority; he knew how to command a room. Nick grew up with parents who did not provide basic necessities for him and his sister. He basically lived out of a U-Haul box in an un-air-conditioned warehouse for many of his formative years (in case that doesn't sound awful enough, here's your friendly reminder that we are above 85 degrees for 8 months out of the year).

He quit school at 15, got married at 17 (not to me), had his first child at 19, the second child at 21, and was divorced at 25. He lived in many different cities, his favorites being Chicago and Milwaukee. He was a garbage man when I met him, working a commercial route after having worked his way through the ranks from residential in different cities for different companies. Garbage was very good to us, and I will never have anything ugly to say about that profession; however, the hours were horrible and it was a pretty smelly job all the way around. It certainly wasn't a stimulating use of Nick's beautiful brain. We always knew Nick was destined for something greater, and the idea for our company kind of sprouted out of a combination of his work as a trash man and my being a commercial property manager. We started our cleaning and maintenance business with a few garbage bags and an $11,000 line of credit co-signed by my dad.

Years passed. The company grew. Nick's midsection grew in direct proportion with his level of stress. He was strong as an ox, but developed hypertension, which ran in his family. He began a pattern of not being able to sleep. We realized he had signs of sleep apnea, but we also knew he was too stubborn to wear a CPAP while he slept. His sleeping patterns worsened, and for the last year of his life (give or take) he slept maybe two consecutive hours each night. The only time he slept soundly was while sitting upright in the shower for maybe thirty minutes at a time…however long he could get the water to stay warm. He'd fall asleep in the bed for a little while, get up and get in the shower, sleep until the cold water awakened him, get back in the bed long enough for the water to reheat, etc.

Nick's burgeoning size definitely contributed to his inability to sleep, and the burgeoning size was a direct result of his work habits. He was the only salesman, he did all the bids, he schmoozed all the clients, and he somehow managed to oversee every job we did. We kept telling ourselves that the work would slow down and we'd be able to hire additional people to help Nick do what he did, but in truth Nick's expectations of people were unrealistic and he liked to micro manage. Basically, he figured nobody would do the job to his satisfaction so he never let anyone try.

Fast forward to the end of July, 2007. We had a strange week at work in that we had a client lunch together every day except for Thursday (I *hated* going to these lunches and Nick knew it…he thought it was funny to make me suffer through four in a single week). On Monday, Nick began to complain of a headache, and he looked really pasty and awful at our lunch that day. He had to go out to a job after dinner that night, and when he came home about three hours later, he ran immediately to the toilet and threw up. We assumed he had food poisoning, so he took a Phenergan we had at home, knowing that's exactly what they'd give him if he went to the emergency room. He knew from previous experience that the Phenergan would give him a headache, but he was feeling so poorly that a mere headache sounded like a walk in the park compared to his overall malaise.

Sure enough, he woke up Tuesday with a headache. He wasn't feeling well, but he blew off his symptoms as relating to the Phenergan he took the night before. Same with Wednesday…he was starting to feel worse, and he thought he might have the flu. By Thursday he was in pretty severe pain, and he finally agreed to stay home and rest. He saw his regular doctor and was diagnosed with a severe sinus infection coupled with an inner ear infection. He was given lots of meds and sent home.

By Friday afternoon he was in tears, which I'd only seen two or three times during our marriage. He asked me to come home from work early that afternoon to take him to the emergency room, which I did. They performed a CT scan in the ER and everything was clear. The docs tried varied combinations of medicines to manage his pain, but nothing was working well. They did several blood tests, and by about 8:00 p.m. he felt slightly better. The doctors were confident in the combo of meds that helped the pain, so they sent us home.

He was eating and cracking jokes and happy for about two hours, which was a relief. He came into our bedroom about 2:00 a.m. (he was sleeping in the guest room and had been for some time because of the snoring…neither of us was sleeping because of it) and woke me up to tell me that the severe pain had returned and he needed me to take him back to the ER. The tears were back. I was groggy from sleep and commented that we didn't have anywhere to take Caroline at that time of the morning. He agreed and said he'd try to stand it a little longer. By 6:30 a.m. he said he'd taken all he could, that he was driving himself to the ER and for me to follow once I got Caro settled with my parents. I was at the hospital with him by 8:00 a.m., and the rounds of testing and trying different meds started again. One doctor commented that he was at a loss, and that his goal was to manage Nick's pain until we could get a neurologist to evaluate his case. They finally admitted him to a room about noon on Saturday.

One of my best friends from forever, Carrie, lives in Sicily but comes home once a year during the summer. She was slated to come home that Saturday night Nick was in the hospital, and he and I were expected at Carrie's parents' house for a party that night. I called them and told them we weren't coming. Nick was in and out of consciousness all day, but he was lucid enough to talk about work and try to eat half of a Subway sandwich CJ brought to him. The doctors ordered an MRI, but poor Nick couldn't fit inside the machine for them to get the test. He came back from the almost-MRI a little down, and I could tell he was exhausted.

I talked to his mom several times throughout the day, along with my good friend, Leslie, my mom, Nick's sister, etc. and assured everyone that Nick would be well once the antibiotics for the sinus infection had time to work. I discouraged everyone from coming to the hospital at Nick's request, because he really felt like he'd be home in a day or two. I asked him if he wanted me to reschedule his Monday appointments, but he was adamant that he'd be better and back to work by then.

Nick insisted that I go with my parents to Carrie's party for a while, and his mom came to sit with him at the hospital for the two hours I was gone. I have had a thousand second guesses on whether or not I should've left him, but Nick was a difficult man with whom to argue. He told me to go and represent our family, so I did. By the time I got back to the hospital, he was totally beat. I tried to get him to eat something, but he was too nauseated. He'd drift off to sleep for a few minutes at a time, and on one such occasion I decided to go downstairs and smoke.

When I came back to the room, I found him out of bed and in the restroom, retching. We called the nurse in and he gave Nick some additional nausea medication. It was close to midnight at this point, so we got Nick back in the bed, I stretched out on the visitor's recliner, and we went to sleep. I heard him snoring, and I remember being shocked that he seemed to be sleeping peacefully for the first time in days. The nurse came back in around 2:00 a.m. to give him his allotted pain meds, and the nurse and I discussed the fact that Nick was actually resting…we were excited! I fell back asleep to the symphony of Nick's snoring until around 4:00 a.m. when the nurse came back in to check his vitals.

Nick had fallen asleep on his side, so the nurse tried to awaken him to roll him onto his back to get a good blood pressure reading. The nurse kind of laughed and said, "Is he normally this hard to wake up?" I smiled and responded that yes, he was a pretty sound sleeper. Then the nurse turned on the overhead light. Nick was blue. The nurse called the code at that point, but Nick was already gone.

They attempted to revive him for over an hour, but he was lost. The doctor told me that Nick never responded in any way to any of the medications or machines used to try and revive him. He was pronounced dead at 5:45 that Sunday morning. So many visions and memories from that point forward. I remember feeling horrible for Nick that his wedding band seemed to be cutting off his circulation; it was so tight on his hand. I remember trying to keep him covered, knowing that he was probably cold, which of course didn't matter anymore.

I called my parents who were luckily close by. Caroline had gone home with Nick's mom the night before, so I didn't have to worry about her care at the time. But I was—within seconds of the doctor's confirming his death—struggling with how to tell them all. The scene was surreal and now, twelve years later, it is still very difficult to think about.

My Mom and Dad

—BY CHANDLER—

My mom raised me to find light in even the darkest people, and to remember that love and equality are two of the most valuable things in life. She would remind me to love people, but still love myself and do what makes me happy. To this day, she still repeats that to me.

When my dad died, Mom and my grandparents became my memory of who he was. They talked about him every day, sharing funny things he did and said. There were photos of him at work, and of Mom and him on vacations together. I hung his portrait close to my desk in our new home.

My earliest memory is when Dad and I were sitting on the hearth in our first house, eating rainbow goldfish. He always pushed the purple ones to the side to eat them last. Now, when I eat rainbow goldfish, I push the purple ones to the side and don't eat them in memory of my dad.

I remember one day when I was only three, dad took me and Mom out on the lake in our boat; we were practically flying with Dad as our captain! I also remember our sucky motor that broke down and left us stranded until a man and woman found us and pulled us back to shore. In a way, it reminds me of how alone I feel sometimes, waving my hands up and down trying to get someone's attention, and how Mom has always been like the people in the other boat. She always knows how to calm me down and fix whatever is wrong.

One of my favorite pictures is of my Dad driving a big motor boat in Gulf Shores, Alabama, where we celebrated my Mema and Papaw's 60th wedding anniversary. I still remember feeling on top of the world, standing at the front of that boat, wind in my hair, like in the movie *Titanic*. I am told Dad loved that day on the water, and I just wish I had been older so I could appreciate it that much more. Sadly, Dad died just two months later. That day at Gulf Shores was the last time I would ever ride in a boat with my dad.

When I first realized I needed to transition to Chandler, I had the initial anxiety any kid would have at the thought of telling their parents. I should have known better than to be scared of telling Mom, though. She was pretty calm and seemed to take it all in stride. Even though I told her several months before I told Mimi and Humbug, it was Mom and Humbug who had the same reaction. They thought it was a phase—after all, who at thirteen could possibly comprehend the weight of that decision? Well, it's been three years since then, and I feel even stronger about it—like I'm finally becoming who I need to be.

My mom realizes now that my gender identity is not a phase. She is *proud* to call me her son, to call me Chandler. So, whether in person or when she posts to Facebook, she refers to me as Chandler (with corresponding pronouns), and people overall have been very accepting of my change. Mom is my rock and my best friend; she is a role model and my hero. I hope one day I can love my kids as much as she loves me. I want my kids to look up to her as much as I do.

Susan "Mimi"
Chandler's Grandmother
—BY SUSAN—

One of the great moments of my life happened June 9, 2003—my first grandchild was born! Until you have experienced this particular miracle, you cannot understand the unspeakable joy that invades your heart. Life has new meaning, new purpose. You have been given another chance to love with all your heart, soul, and mind.

My days were filled with thoughts of Caroline, and how I might help her mom and dad raise her. This overwhelming joy I experienced in my new role as grandmother took me somewhat by surprise. I wanted to be involved more than I would have imagined, and thankfully, Ashlea was most happy to let me share in all the important moments.

Ashlea and Nick started their own business nine months after Caroline was born, so I became more involved. Since I owned my own business, they hired a sweet nanny to help out three days a week. Their company grew, and life was moving at a swift pace for all of us. We had birthday parties by our pool, and celebrated all our holidays together. One of the most special family events was being together to see Nick baptized by an old friend of the family. It was just a couple of years after his baptism when this same pastor spoke at Nick's memorial service. Another two years passed when we watched as Caroline was baptized at only six years of age. Time did bring us new joy.

When Caroline was three, I had an idea to invite about 50 children and their mothers to a Mad Hatter's Tea Party. We served fancy tea sandwiches, pink lemonade, Easter egg petits fours, and a beautiful cake shaped like a teapot. Fresh florals in teapots centered several round tables dressed with floor-length tablecloths of pink or lime green. Small ceramic egg pedestals filled with mini jelly beans sat atop each place setting. Sheer pink panels were tied into bows on the back of each white garden chair.

My sister even agreed to dress up as the Mad Hatter and greet the guests as they entered under an Easter Egg & Bunny trellis. On this perfectly cool, blue-sky Good Friday morning, my nephew hid 400 eggs among the stone walkways, ivy, trees, and azaleas. We had giant eggs in the gardens, a teapot piñata on a May pole, prizes, and magic was in the air!

Yes, those were the days of thrills and excitement. Unfortunately, Caroline's June birthday would mark her last one with her daddy, as Nick was taken from us less than two months later. It was so sudden and unexpected and devastating to us all; it took several months to find some semblance of balance. Caroline was only four at the time, so her comprehension of the permanency of separation from her dad would come later.

Caroline continued to grow. She loved winning races against boys and could always throw a football or baseball "like a boy." She would try different organized sports, but seemed to get hurt a lot. Many times, the injuries were related to growth plate issues, similar to what had happened with my own children. It was frustrating, just as it had been when mine were growing up—the very thing they enjoyed and that would help keep them fit was denied by injuries. Consequently, they watched TV and ate!

There were the mundane chores of carpool, homework and such, as we poured ourselves into young Caroline's life. It was obvious (to us) that our grandchild was bright, but like so many children, Caroline had a fear of math. We worked hard on it, and spent several summers with workbooks, flash cards, games, etc. There were tears, and then came moments of clarity when we thought the fear and confusion had vanquished. Finally, after a full year of Kumon repetitive study, the multiplication tables were conquered. Could there be anything harder than that in raising Caroline? Fast forward to middle school and puberty; and the answer is *yes*.

MY FAITH

—BY SUSAN—

Before the next section of this book, "The Journey," allow me to share with you that I've had a Biblical world view since I was a child. By that, I mean that everything that has happened to me in life, both good and bad, has been viewed through the lens of faith in a great God who made Himself known to me when I was only eight years old. I believe in the Trinity, the *Triune God*. As I trusted **Jesus** (Son of **God** Incarnate, God *in the flesh*) to be my Master and Savior, and sought Him (God the **Holy Spirit** living in me) to guide me through life, I learned four very simple, but profound Truths:

He knows it all

He made it all

He loves us all

He forgives us all

Think about each one. Now, knowing these truths and believing 100% in them does not prevent me from going my own way occasionally—like, every day. Let me be completely honest with you. The greatest paradox of my life is that I will never be able to live up to my desire to be what God wants me to be. That is, not now—on this earth, in this fleshly body, with this highly distractible mind.

It's true, I cannot do it. But what if I told you that God knew all along this would be true for me and every other human being? The Bible says we are <u>credited</u> with <u>righteousness</u> (transgressions forgiven, sins covered) when we believe that God raised Jesus from the dead—delivered Him over to death for our sins, and raised Him to life for our justification.

That means we did nothing to deserve this ongoing forgiveness that we receive—debt paid—simply by believing. Check out Romans 4 in the New Testament. Verse 25 says *"He (Jesus) was handed over to die because of our sins, and He was raised to life to make us right with God."* God knew that when we really "get" the idea of the freedom in His Gift of Redemption, it will cause us to yearn to do things His way.

These facts and many transforming moments with God prepared me to write and publish a devotional book called *First Fruits* in January 2016. I will explain in "The Struggle" section of this book just how our grandchild's news impacted my spiritual life, and how God led me to once again rely on Him.

CJ "Humbug"
Chandler's Grandfather
—BY SUSAN—

CJ is the patriarch of the family and grandfather to his first-born, whom he now dutifully tries to call Chandler. We will get to his struggle later, but for now, just remember that Humbug and his Caroline were buddies. They swam, fished with Roux (his Boykin Spaniel hunting dog), slurped watermelon, and took naps together.

Humbug and I both grew up in Louisiana, raised in middle-class, conservative homes. We met at college, married, and moved to Texas after CJ graduated. He taught Physical Science and Biology, and coached football and track for five years at a large high school in Houston. He then managed various commercial real estate groups for 32 years. For the last few years he has been selling commercial electricity to many of the same managers he used to employ.

Humbug always tried to stay away from "the fray" when we females were hormonal—he'd walk out the door and tell us he was "going to see a man about a dog" when he thought "too much estrogen was flying around." It didn't matter if we were happy, excited, or in a fuss over something—he tried to avoid these moments at all costs. And to prove the point, one day soon after Caroline was born, he *did* go see a man about a dog—and that's how he got his first Boykin Spaniel which he named Roux, in honor of his gumbo-loving Louisiana heritage.

This man grew up hunting and fishing, and paid a king's ransom to have Roux trained to pick up birds. She never did catch a flying fish, though she had enough heart to try if Humbug had ever taken her on a real fishing trip. All in all, Roux picked up 962 ducks over 12 years of hunting. Now, it's up to Deuce (named Roux II) who's going through the same rigorous training—she's pretty high strung, being a model bird dog, so she may be good for a thousand.

CJ has a big heart and grew up in a Christian home. He and I met at a Christian college, and patterned our lives with God a part of everyday conversation. Over the last twenty years, faith has become more important to us as we see the world changing and realize the impact it will have on our children and grandchildren. CJ now leads a Coaches Outreach Bible Study for all the coaching staff at a large high school in our community. He has a gift for connecting with men, and especially coaches since he was a coach himself.

Our marriage has taken some twists and turns, had some mountaintops as well as some valleys, some hilarity and some gravity. There were moments when I knew with certainty why God put us together when I was only 20, and other times when I couldn't think of one good reason for why we've stayed together all these years. We celebrated 50 years of marriage on July 13, 2018, and for the life of me, I can't imagine how we could have been married for that long. Many of the bumps in the road that should have shaken us apart, had just the opposite effect as they held us together. There is only one answer for this phenomenon, and it is God. He has been our glue.

The Journey

Puberty

—BY SUSAN—

Most of us who have been through puberty would agree that it is a time of self-critique. Teens view themselves through a microscope, finding flaws in both their body and their personality. Many are fortunate enough to have confidence in the love and acceptance of their family, but are now venturing more into the social world of friends, where they are anxious to be accepted and loved.

There is an awkwardness inside these adolescents who hope and pray no one can see how they really feel. They either go quietly through their day, or put on a façade of confidence that can be crushed with a single look or comment. The hormones surging through their young bodies are causing emotional ups and downs, not to mention outward evidence of how they are changing from children to young adults.

"Other than dying, I think puberty is probably about as rough as it gets." This quote from 80s music icon Rick Springfield may be overstated, but the reality of the emotional pain kids experience is real. The good news is, it doesn't have to last forever, even when it feels as though it will … like Winston Churchill said, "If you're going through hell, keep going!"

Looking back at Caroline's middle school years, there were signs of a growing angst in sixth grade, but we weren't sure it was anything abnormal. Like childbirth or a root canal, who wants to dwell on the pain? She was moving away from wanting to be hugged or given love pats, but since I could still remember steering clear of parental affection when I was a teen, we thought most of this was normal.

As we were soon to understand, Caroline's behavior was far from normal. She was going down a rabbit hole of self-hatred and doubt, coupled with an inability to understand or express those feelings in a healthy manner.

"Am I Allowed to Like Girls?"
—BY CHANDLER—

A few years after my dad passed, my mom began dating and met a group of actors through one of the guys she dated. Even after that relationship ended, these guys remained friends and became some of the most influential and lovable people I have ever had the honor to know. They are great at encouraging me— funny, and super loyal to both Mom and me. I refer to them as my "Guncles." They were my first introduction to gay men, and I've never met such supportive and protective people outside my real family.

But they were gay *men*; with me still looking like a girl at this point, I had not yet met another girl who liked girls. Yes, I thought that girls dating girls was the same as guys dating guys, but for some reason I didn't see myself under the category of lesbian. Yet, as I got older, I found myself straying farther and farther away from ever seeing myself liking guys.

The summer before I started middle school, the word 'transgender' was not in my vocabulary, so I told my mom I was bisexual and liked both boys and girls. It was common to talk about sexual things with my friends, and I guess we were all trying to figure ourselves out. I was not positive that I was a lesbian, but I knew I was attracted to girls.

Then, in the middle of seventh grade, halfway through middle school, I told my mom I was a lesbian. Both times I told her I liked someone other than a guy, she told me the same exact thing: "Don't bring this up to Mimi and Humbug right now," so I didn't. Even though I told her about these changes in my sexuality, it still didn't feel completely accurate. I would later discover what did feel exactly right for me—and the price to be paid for that discovery.

Cutting

—BY SUSAN—

Before we move forward to Chandler's revelation, I must tell you about the precursor—months of self-loathing and self-harm. Caroline was living a life of quiet desperation during the onset of cutting. When Ashlea discovered the cuts on her child, she took Caroline to a therapist, but was trying to handle it as a single parent without involving CJ and me.

Ashlea eventually let us know, but she hoped Caroline's cutting was under control. It was at least happening less frequently. Ashlea warned Caroline that she might have to be admitted to a hospital if the cutting continued, and that fear of leaving home seemed to stem the tide. As much as CJ and I tried to listen to Caroline and give her attention, we had no idea what was causing the depression. Any disagreement with her friends sent her into a tailspin, and we were all ill-equipped to handle it. We were particularly disturbed one morning when we witnessed the results of her cutting the night before in our own home. Caroline had spent the night with us, and I worried that I might have said something to cause it.

The seeds of discontent and self-hatred were growing stronger each time Caroline resorted to cutting. She had become a different person than the cheerful child of the past. There was a growing obsession with her girlfriends, one in particular, that kept her upset. Ashlea tried separating them, but it seemed to make things worse over several months, so they were finally allowed to spend time together once again. Chandler now admits this friend was more than just a friend. That thought flit through my mind briefly, but remembering how much I loved my girlfriends at that age, I brushed it aside.

As stated earlier, the dress code of choice was basketball shorts and tees. Dresses were for "girly-girls," and this kid did not want any part of it. Then, out of the blue, in January of 2016, her sixth-grade year, she changed—we began to see Caroline in dresses; lips and eyes became more prominent with impeccably-applied makeup. She was beautiful. Photos and selfies were ablaze, and Caroline began sharing with us all the great compliments she was getting on Instagram.

This lasted just a few months, then the shorts and tees were back. At least the cutting stopped as abruptly as it started. Caroline found healthier ways to deal with her feelings.

Reality Check

—BY SUSAN—

By springtime of 2016, Caroline recalled she didn't feel complete—like there was something missing. She began doing some research on sexual orientation and discovered the word *transgender.* Caroline felt like it was describing her. It means to have the desire to be the opposite gender from the gender you were born with. Another new word, *dysphoria,* meant an utter hatred and disgust of one's body. Caroline said she felt like she had finally found a description of how she felt inside.

By mid-summer, I finally faced the truth. We were not getting along, and I struggled to endure what seemed like ungratefulness and disrespect as I navigated the uncharted waters of realizing my granddaughter was changing. At first, it seemed like teenage rebellion, so I prayed for patience. I then realized it was something much deeper, and that Caroline was screaming in silence as she began to pull away from me.

So, after spending a few days with Caroline in my hometown, I came back home and asked Ashlea if we could have a one-on-one. The weekend had gone badly between Caroline and me, which caused my emotions to swing between anger and depression. Where was my sweet granddaughter with whom I had always gotten along? I asked Ashlea to confirm to me that the problem had to do with Caroline wanting to be a boy—to which I received a sober "yes."

Caroline and I went to lunch the next day, and she tried to explain to me how she had been feeling and what she had found out in her research. I was shocked at how much information she had retained and how well she grasped it all. My plan that day was to mainly listen, and try to absorb all she wanted to share. Caroline had commented at the outset that she just wanted me to be her grandma—not her teacher or her preacher.

I decided rather than make a lot of comments I might later regret, I would ask just one question. So, when she finished sharing, I asked Caroline how she had reconciled her feelings and desires with God's Word and His will. She questioned my meaning, so I told her I wanted to know if she had figured out what God thinks about what she wanted. She told me she guessed she hadn't done that. Caroline was too raw emotionally for me to try to explain God's plan, and frankly, I was pretty raw myself. Besides, I had already been told I was not to be her preacher.

Coming Out as Chandler

—BY SUSAN—

In April of 2016, several months before I found out, Caroline came out to her mom about being transgender. Her mom noticed some references to *Chandler* on Caroline's Instagram account, but thought it just a nickname. In truth, this was just a segue to her new name—something she decided upon with friends late in seventh grade. Her close friends had begun calling her Chandler.

Caroline celebrated her 13th birthday in June 2016. She went in the salon as Caroline with a ponytail—and out the door as Chandler with a full-on boy cut, buzzed on the sides and back. She seemed happier than we had seen her in a while, and she surprised all her friends with her new look at her birthday party. Though I would find out about this new name a few months later, the kids must have been warned not to say Chandler when I was around.

The summer after seventh grade, Caroline was openly talking with the family about getting fit. [It's important to note that we were always involved in the *pursuit* of a sport for Caroline: softball, tennis, swimming, basketball, running, Taekwondo and finally, weight training.] We went to the gym almost every day that summer, and she was back in the clothes she loved: shorts, tees, and tennis shoes. There seemed to be an unusual drive to lift more weights and become strong. She did some cardio and lost some weight, but the focus was on machines that required heavy lifting.

When eighth grade began, "Caroline" began introducing himself to new students and teachers as Chandler. And, of course, he now seemed to fit the style of clothing he had preferred all along. Interestingly, everyone (including teachers and the administrative staff at school) adapted to Chandler's new look and name as if it had always been so. We sensed a new positive outlook in him and were so relieved that cutting had become a thing of the past.

Chandler was in varsity choir, and had always been comfortable just singing ensemble. But this year, he decided to join theater as well as choir, and try out for the fall musical, *Hairspray*. New confidence came oozing out of him as the parts were announced and Chandler got a starring role as Edna Turnblad. Other parts came his way throughout the year, and by the spring theater banquet, Chandler had won the honor of Best Actor.

In addition, Chandler won Vocalist of the Year in choir. Equally important, the math that had plagued him for his entire school experience had suddenly been conquered with the help of a math teacher who encouraged him and helped him believe in himself. He won an award for excellence in math as he made the highest scoring difference from his district on the math portion of the Texas STAAR test. Chandler seemed to have a new vision for himself that colored everything he did! Color, indeed, as Chandler began to sketch all sorts of animals, faces, symbols, etc. with an ability beyond anything we had ever witnessed in him. He said it calmed him, and seemed nonplussed by it. Eighth grade turned out to be a banner year for Chandler.

We would all soon learn that those accolades were a cushion of common ground for what lay ahead. Our family celebrated Chan's accomplishments, but struggled to find balance in the heat of conflict and change. Ashlea and Chandler brought a united front of confidence concerning Chandler's desire to embrace life as a transgender male. Our position of faith and love would be challenged, and somewhat dismissed, as we navigated uncharted waters of familial discontent.

45

The Struggle

Life with Mimi (Susan)

—BY CHANDLER—

When I was growing up, I spent every day of every summer at Mimi and Humbug's house. It was like a vacation for me that was only five minutes away. But as I grew and changed and started facing the fact that I was not going to be the little "girly-girl" that Mimi wanted, it made everything harder. Because we were connected at the hip and I told her everything, I simply hated lying to her. It felt like my stomach was imploding. As I got older, it formed into a very bad habit that I sadly was not allowed to break.

Mimi grew me up praying at every meal and using God as her comparison to scenarios that I went through. Like, if I was struggling with a friend for example, one of her immediate responses, if not her only one, was to pray. Though praying never helped me, I would lie and say it did, and that I felt ten times better from having prayed. That was the first thing I became accustomed to lying about.

Then, it was lying about a boy liking me. What she and every other person in my family did not know was that guys never liked me as anything more than "one of the guys." Before I knew it, I was lying to her about everything—even things I did not have to lie about. This ball of hatred and disgust was forming around this woman who helped raise me. I did not know how to stop it, and a part of me did not really want to.

By mid-seventh grade, these feelings progressed in the worst possible way, up until just a couple of months before eighth grade ended. When I "came out" to my mom about changing my name to Chandler, I knew Mimi was the next person who deserved to know. When we sat down at a restaurant to talk about things, I started rambling and beating around the bush about being transgender— but, she already knew. I did not even have to tell her fully. I thought she took it pretty well, but then again, I forgot she knew how to lie just as well as I did . . .

Later on, I distinctly remember the thing she said to me that made me think, "I may not be able to keep her in my life." It was only a few months after I told her that her granddaughter of thirteen years wanted to become her grandson. Mimi had given up on hiding the inner war between love and faith, and was spewing it out onto everyone around her. I had just started eighth grade and was making new friends as "Chandler" through theater class. I had just been cast as a main character in the school musical, and of course, Mom and Mimi wanted to help make it the best it could be. Just when I thought I was actually going to be okay, I was told she had spread her emotions about me to my best friends and class members. I had been working my butt off for this show we were all in together.

I was in the middle of a dance number when a friend told me what she said—I was hit with this ball of rage that filled up my stomach and was spreading faster than a forest fire through my lungs and up into my esophagus. The only thing I heard from my then best friend, before I went into shock was hearing that Mimi said, "I know what is going on; you can call her Chandler, but that does not mean I ever will."

I truly did try to hold in every ounce of anger that had formed in my body, but I was too furious. I was angry for one reason mainly—that she had the audacity to say something she had no room to say in front of the people that I wanted as friends, but were not that close with yet. I still remember the look of pure disgust I gave her after rehearsal, but I was the one that ended up being yelled at by Mom, because I was forgetting how much time, money, and effort Mimi put in to making *Hairspray* a success.

I did not listen, though, when Mimi continued to scream in the car and say, "I WILL NEVER CALL YOU CHANDLER! YOUR NAME IS CAROLINE! THAT IS THE NAME YOU WERE BORN WITH!" I did not listen or care because I had already made up my mind that she did not deserve me in her life. As time went on, things got worse. I stopped eating as much and my heart formed a habit of hating her.

For a while I stopped visiting, and I was okay with it until I noticed how much it hurt my mom. But what I hated was that when I was at my worst with Mimi, all I could talk about with Mom was how much I despised my own grandma. I remember thinking it would never get better.

Almost three-quarters of the way through eighth grade, Mimi started seeing the pain I had been hiding. Mom and I had moved in with Mimi and Humbug at the end of February while mom looked for another job. At this point, my body and mind were growing tired of hiding the pain that came from hearing "Caroline" and their "precious little girl." It got to the point where I could simply walk into their house and get this massive headache, like I was being strangled. I never realized it was because I needed to cry. I needed to tell them how awful they were making me feel, the pain now coming from both Mimi and Humbug.

One Sunday night, I got the chance to tell them every excruciating detail about my life the past year. I screamed and cried and was finally able to tell them how heartbroken I was, and how they were so blinded by their faith to even consider that maybe, just maybe, I deserved an equal chance to be Chandler like they deserved an equal chance to be right. All of that anger and sadness had broken me, and screaming and crying was my own personal ibuprofen.

Susan Butler

Life with Humbug (CJ)
—BY CHANDLER—

When I think of a grandfather, I think of the old guy that helps you string the line through your first fishing pole, and takes you for ice cream when your mom and grandma say not to. When I hear the word "grandpa" I think of a second dad.

Since my dad died when I was so young, I think my mom really hoped that I would get taken under Humbug's wing to show me all the things my dad would have shown me. For years, Humbug and I were best buds. He made me the best grilled cheese in the world, and told me facts about science that helped me in no way, but made him happy. As they say, "once a teacher, always a teacher."

Humbug is a hunter and a fisherman. He grabs his hunting dog by the ear and drags her until she squeals as a form of teaching, but his love for her is never in question. I have also never questioned his love for his family. He may not be able to express his love verbally, but he shares his love for us through cooking and fun trips he takes us on.

Then there is me, living my life at the total opposite end of the spectrum. For starters, I am an actor and a singer, so I enjoy creative expression. Whereas Humbug's walls in his study are filled with stuffed ducks, my walls are covered with movie posters and theater awards. There are things we do meet in the middle on, though, like our deep-rooted need for really clean eye glasses since we are two of the blindest people in the family.

For years, I have worn Humbug's basketball shorts when I come over and claimed them as my own—so much so that he doesn't even notice anymore. He did, however, lay subtle claim to his shorts last Christmas by getting me a couple pair of my own with a CJP monogram. That was actually cool!

I have grown up with a liberal mom who taught me about equality, and introduced me to social and political issues I didn't even know were a thing. I think what bothered me the most about Humbug was that he believed the exact opposite of everything I believed. To give you a visual, if there was a "Build Your Own Trump Supporter" app for iPhone, Humbug would be the poster child. Then there's me, his trans grandkid. So, that said, when Caroline became Chandler, Humbug did not handle it well.

Something to note about my grandfather is that he does not talk about things that push him out of his comfort zone. My girlfriend of several months was at the house one night and Humbug still called her my 'friend', thus proving my point. He has the mindset of "maybe if I don't bring it up, it will go away," which I have had to get used to. I have had to do everything in my power to remind myself that good things take time…lots and lots of time.

Now, did I ever plan on him throwing me a "So Happy You're Becoming a Boy" party? NO! But I never in a million years expected him to stoop so low that he became just as bad as some of the guys at school. The day Humbug called me "it" was the day my respect for him stopped creeping out of the window, and instead made a run for it. I may not agree with him on much, and my youth may have blinded me from some of his truth, but no matter how little we share or how much he disagrees with how I feel, the word "it" should have never left his lips. That's not just because we are family; it's because there has to be a shared level of common decency in any relationship.

You have to remember my mom was always a daddy's girl, whereas I was always a momma's boy. So, when Mom saw my lack of respect for him escalating, she hated it more than I have ever seen her hate anything. In my view, he lives on this pedestal where he gets babied and protected simply because he "pays the bills." As I get older, I hope to be able to understand his mental blocks for this situation, because there have been times when I thought he hated me.

Here is how a normal argument with Humbug goes. Keep in mind that he is 73 and tends to think he is right when it comes to political and social stuff. He is a man that just happened to grow up in a completely different era where racism was accepted and "gay" meant happy. So, he says what he thinks and claims it to be fact. Humbug can make a comment about anything from Trump to AIDS to thinking so poorly of his own grandchild that he has cause to call me "it."

My mom and my grandma pass over a lot of his comments, always giving him a pass because he has "low testosterone levels" or because "that's just how he is and we can't change him." Then one of the women in the family steps in (most likely my mom if she's around, but Mimi steps in a lot more now than she used to) and they beef it out right there at the dinner table, or when Fox News goes to commercial. Around this time, someone stops talking because they are wound so tightly and are so full of anger that the room gets really quiet until I change the subject. Normally, I don't speak out when I disagree with Humbug simply because I know how much it upsets Mom; though lately, I haven't felt I had much choice. People cannot hide their bigotry behind their age; it's just a number.

Sometimes I feel like I'm trapped in a big glass box, where I'm talking but no one can hear me. I want my voice to be heard and respected just as much as Humbug's voice is. My Uncle Bart and his family came in for Thanksgiving this year, and Humbug brought all the equipment to do a fish fry at our house since these relatives hadn't been to our new house. Humbug and I fried the fish and hushpuppies on the back porch, and for the first time, I could actually see that he was trying to call me Chan and use the correct pronouns. It gave me hope that he might see a better relationship beginning because of his willingness to do something that was uncomfortable for him, but right for me.

I just want the people I love to love me back, and to care about my feelings enough to understand that I am still the person they have always loved. I may begin to look and sound different, but I will always be that kid who loves to joke around, enter into discussions about current events, get to know my teachers, enjoy my friends and family, and strive to be the best human being I can be.

54

Feuds—Frustration—Fasting—Forgiveness

—BY SUSAN—

The overarching theme of this saga is *misunderstanding.* I will never know if, given the chance, we could all do it better. But, let it be a warning—when we experience actions and reactions from a loved one that we are unaccustomed to, we need to investigate until we get to the truth. Why is this person acting so unlike themselves? Why am I feeling guilty when I don't know what I have done? When did things change, and was there any outside force influencing the change? We need to have the courage to ask the hard questions.

I drove myself crazy with unanswered questions once I came face to face with the transgender reality. I would have flashes of anger at Caroline, until I realized I was really angry at God. I hurt for Caroline, knowing the rough water ahead of her in trying to navigate life as a transgender boy. How could this happen to our precious child? It all seemed so unreal.

The most painful part *spiritually* for me had to do with the timing of it. Why did God allow this to happen so soon after my first book had been published? I had labored to write a 480-page devotional book over the course of 3-1/2 years to testify for my Savior. Different special friends had given me five beautiful book signing events to launch *First Fruits* that spring of 2016. I was on the path of my purpose to share Christ's love with the world. Why now, Lord?

You see, I had already accepted the fact that there would be a price to pay for being bold in my faith, even before I wrote *First Fruits* …

1 Peter 4:12-13 (NASB):

12"Beloved, do not be surprised at the fiery ordeal among you, which comes upon you for your testing, as though some strange thing were happening to you; 13but to the degree that you share the sufferings of Christ, keep on rejoicing, so that also at the revelation of His glory you

Susan Butler

may rejoice with exultation. [14]If you are reviled for the name of Christ,
you are blessed, because the Spirit of glory and of God rests on you."

Satan seemed to hang around quite often during the *First Fruits* writing sessions with words of self-defeat. And now, after persevering to get the book completed and published, here he was again gnawing at me … would people think my faith was fake because I couldn't even raise up my children in the faith? How would I be able to speak out for Christ with this dark secret dragging me into the abyss? I didn't understand transgender yet—it seemed so shameful. I was heartbroken.

Feuds

The summer after 7th grade, I noticed a significant change in Caroline. This was the summer Caroline was going to get fit, so we committed to work out at the gym five days a week. At first, it was going well and I tried to encourage Caroline with praise and a high-five each time we completed our circuits.

Gradually, I realized Caroline was finishing before me, and would sit at the front to wait for me. It seemed the enthusiasm was waning. Though she had asked me to remind her of her commitment to better eating habits, there was obvious resentment when I did so. (I get it – it's a challenge every day for me to make good food choices.)

The atmosphere when Caroline was around could change in a flash. We called her Sybil from the time she was just a few months old (remember the old movie about the woman with multiple personalities?). We laughed about it when she was young, but as she got older, the brooding and anger had become something in which we found no humor. We never knew what mood to expect. Though the highs were great fun with smiles and laughter, the dark side could show up without warning. Ashlea finally resorted to asking Caroline to leave the room until she could find her way back to some sense of normal.

By the time we went to my hometown mid-summer of 2016, Caroline got angry and sullen from the moment we drove off in the car (rather than the truck which she had expected). She didn't know we were forced to drive the sedan because of impending rain—all she thought about was her already 5'8" frame and how cramped she would be. We understood, but we preferred to have dry luggage when we arrived. By the time we took a restroom break, I had had it with her attitude, and told her so. That conversation became known as the "green gas" analogy. I told her that every time she got mad about something, she would get "all puffed up and quiet—and that it felt like this negative *green gas* was invading the atmosphere."

We shared a hotel room, and except for one moment of levity when I had to help her use a zit remover, she spoke to me only when she had to. When we were with the family, she stayed as far away from me as possible. I couldn't say or do anything right in her eyes.

The plan was for her to go back to San Antonio with my sister for a few days. Believe me, CJ and I were looking forward to that as much as Caroline was. We drove home listening to music and talking about the weekend (where my brother had debuted with a new band at an LSUS balloon festival). Meanwhile, my sister was getting an earful of *green gas* on their way home, all directed at yours truly. During Caroline's stay, she told my sister and my sister's close friend about wanting to become a boy, and that she dreaded telling me.

Frustration

As you have already learned from Caroline, we were so close all those years, and had never had any secrets *that I knew of.* Man, was that assumption getting ready to be blown out of the water. I was devastated that Caroline chose to share her problems with my sister rather than with me. Not only had she shared about her cutting the year before, but now this transgender news as well. I understood that my sister was a buffer in Caroline's mind, but it still hurt.

I had always told Caroline I would do anything for her, even down to giving my life for her. And I meant it. But, in Caroline's mind, I wonder if she questioned not whether I would *die* for her, but would I *live* for her and support her as a transgender boy named Chandler? Could I make the adjustment from all things pink and girly to a boy with a deepening voice, whiskers, and girlfriends?

I'm sad to say Caroline had reason to question my aptitude for this Herculean challenge. I had been quite vocal when Bruce Jenner came out as Caitlyn. So, round one was a knock-out punch, when I was barraged by her friends and the theater director at rehearsal one afternoon. Without warning, I heard them call my Caroline by what she had chosen as her new name—Chandler. Chandler's recall of that event was spot on. I did pronounce to her friends at rehearsal and on the way home in the car to my grandchild that I would NEVER call her anything but Caroline. I was self-righteous and livid at the thought of this sea change of events.

Do you want to know when I fully realized just how hurtful that scene was? Not at the Sunday night revelation where Chandler poured his heart out, or even what I did after the revelation (read on). It was after I asked Chandler to take part in this story by sharing his viewpoint, and *read* what he wrote. For the first time, I could feel not just his *anger,* but his *pain* in reliving that moment at school. Though I was not privy to the planning stages of his name change, or the fact that most of his friends had been calling him Chandler for months, it was obvious I had hurt him.

When I heard them call him Chandler that very first time, the word hit me with brute force, and I reacted with barely-hidden fury. I just could not accept that my only granddaughter was making such a radical change.

I'm ashamed of the selfish pronouncement which I thought, at the time, was very principled, courageous, and noble. It was, in fact, unkind.

Fasting

The Sunday night revelation happened quite by accident … if you believe in the randomness of events which can change the course of history. As a believer in the sovereignty of God and His promise to work all things together for good to those who love the Lord and are called to His purpose—I believe it was God's timing.

Revelation One

A couple of weeks before Caroline's revelation, God revealed a message to me while watching the movie *"The Shack."* The story is about a family man who takes his two daughters and one son camping. The next morning, the youngest daughter is kidnapped and subsequently murdered. This story depicts God the Father, His Son Jesus, and the Holy Spirit as three surprisingly uncharacteristic individuals with different genders and ethnicities (the writer's attempt to remove stereotypical images of God).

The time comes in the story for God to take the dad up to a cave to view the scene of the crime and his daughter's bones. Not only does the dad have to face the horror of envisioning his little girl's terror and pain, but he is now encouraged by God to think about the murderer's own pain—what he might have experienced as a child, and what led him to the moment where he stepped from the bounds of human kindness into the pit of a deranged mad man. This murderer was once an innocent little boy—just like the daddy's little girl.

And then, the last requirement, the unthinkable … Forgiveness. "No!" the dad screamed. "I'm justified in hating him! He took my baby girl! He doesn't deserve forgiveness—You can't expect me to forgive this guy!" (paraphrased). As he agonized and fought against the idea through a river of tears, God infused this broken man with His Spirit of Peace and Love—and the dad forgave.

When this scene was over, I was breathless, my head pulsating with every beat of my pounding heart. I heard in my spirit a voice saying, "Susan, remember this. I am going to teach you things you have not known. Hard things. Our walk together in *First Fruits* was just the beginning … there is much more to learn through Caroline."

Caroline's quiet rage had been building after Caroline and Ashlea moved in with us. She avoided looking me in the eye when I tried to talk to her, and went straight to her room after school each day. I was frustrated in warring between the love I so wanted to demonstrate, and my faith which seemingly prevented me from accepting Caroline's compulsion to change her gender identity.

Caroline and I had talked many times about ignoring friends rather than retaliating. I told her that sometimes the best way to get your point across to someone who has offended you is to ignore them for a while. She had tested the theory and knew it to be true. In my mind, it was better than saying something to the person you might regret later. As it turned out, I was getting a big dose of my own advice.

I began praying harder for the Lord to reveal to me His will in this difficult situation. Surely it wasn't His will for my grandchild and me to be at such odds. It is human nature to ask "why" when trials come from which we cannot escape or understand. We were no exception when this transgender issue arose. God began to nudge me about fasting—something I had never disciplined myself to do.

I then came upon the scripture concerning a woman possessed by demons. Jesus told His disciples that some issues took more than prayer; some took prayer and fasting. Though I didn't think Caroline was demon-possessed, I did believe Satan was prowling around like a roaring lion seeking whom to devour (1 Peter 5:8 NASB). It occurred to me that *he is not satisfied with destroying the character of adults only, but he wants to take the hearts of our children.* All he has to do is distract them with the world's view of happiness, and keep them from God's truth about His purpose for their lives.

Revelation Two

So, on the Sunday night of Caroline's revelation, I was already set to fast Monday at sunrise through Wednesday at sundown, though I had told no one. I had gone to Ashlea's room to ask a question, and Caroline was in there. We began a casual conversation which escalated quickly into Caroline's revelation of her feelings. I called CJ into the bedroom with us, feeling a quickening in my heart that this was a moment of huge import.

We sat there and listened to Caroline as she struggled to tell us of the pain she had been feeling because of our inability to accept her as Chandler. She told how great she felt at school, and then how a horrible feeling of depression and sadness would come over her as she walked into our house after school. She said it was just too hard to be with us when we didn't understand her needs. CJ and I had already been confronted with articles and a documentary concerning the high suicide rate for transgender people, and now understood from the obvious pain in her voice that we had to formulate a drastic new approach.

Before I got out of bed the next morning, I began praying with my whole heart that God would reveal Himself to me as I sought Him with prayer and fasting. I confessed that I did not have confidence in myself to complete three days, but that I was trusting Him to guide me through. It was apparent before my feet hit the floor that God was already at work, telling me to lean into Caroline and love her.

Caroline went to school early that morning, CJ was in his office, and I stopped by Ashlea's room to let her know that I was going to go into Caroline's room to pray. I went in and shut the door, then sat in an old French chair I had bought from a dear friend's family after she passed. She had been a spiritual mentor to me, and I now think how comforting it was that a bit of her was in the room.

I began by thanking God for His mighty power and love for me and for Caroline. I thanked Him for His direction that had led me to be in Caroline's room that morning. I thanked Him for Caroline. What a special gift He had given us more than 13 years before. I knew He surely was not finished with her, and neither was I.

I asked God to bless every piece of clothing, furniture, and surface that Caroline would touch, and that Satan be bound from our home and from this room. I asked Him to protect Caroline's mind and heart from the evil one, and to give her direction and hope for the future. There were so many things to speak of concerning Caroline, so I spent close to an hour talking with the Lord about our beloved grandchild.

In researching fasting, and because I'd just been diagnosed as prediabetic, my fast would consist of water, broth, tea and juices—no meals to look forward to—yikes! Adjusting to this regimen the first day was not too difficult, amazingly, so I spent my time drinking juices, meditating on scripture, walking in my back yard, and praying.

By afternoon as school ended, I was back at my desk in our master bedroom doing some Bible study. As I mentioned, Caroline had formed a habit of going straight to her room after school. This day, something different happened … Caroline opened the door to my bedroom and said, "Hi, Mimi. Mom says you're doing some kind of fast?" As she was saying this, I had swiveled my chair around, stood smiling and said for the very first time, "Hi, Chandler" with open arms. With eyes bright and a big smile, Chandler rushed into my arms for a long, wonderful hug! The Lord had given me peace to begin calling our grandchild Chandler, and Chandler's reaction was confirmation. That hug had been months in the making— what a moment!

I went to sleep that night with a smile on my face. The next morning as I greeted the Lord before I got up, I asked Him about the agenda for the day. I heard His voice again: "Wash Chandler's clothes." So, I got up and told Ashlea what I was going to do. Her response was that I make sure Chandler knew this was just a one-time deal (since Ashlea had given that chore to Caroline a couple of years before). I told Ashlea if it was okay with her, I felt the Lord leading me to continue washing and folding Chandler's clothes for the duration of their time with us. It would be my love language.

I spent the day doing laundry, praying, and resting in between loads. This second day was harder, and I was glad for it to end. However, I did enjoy getting to surprise Chandler with all the organized stacks of folded clothes. The guest room was cramped, so keeping his stuff organized was a necessity. Order makes people feel better, even when they may not realize it.

Day three, Wednesday, was a great day. I continued with my prayer and fasting, and thanked the Lord for answering my prayers as I trusted Him to guide me through the days. One thing I have learned is that it's not necessary to talk constantly when you pray. God has things to reveal to us, and He can't do that if we are talking the whole time. Meditating and asking God to reveal Himself to us is an act I am certain pleases God.

Psalm 37:4 (NASB):
"Delight yourself in the Lord, and He will give
you the desires of your heart."

My primary take-away from the fasting experience was:
TRUST God
LOVE Chandler

These precepts may seem simplistic, even obvious, but the doing is far from simple. It is challenging when you know your child is headed for deep water. The good news is that we have a Life Preserver in Jesus Christ, primed and ready. We just have to let go of our doubts and insecurities, and hold on to *His* life line.

I am reminded just now of an old hymn we used to sing when I was a child called *"Throw Out the Life Line."* Read the chorus and last verse:

Throw out the life line! Throw out the life line!
Someone is drifting away,
Throw out the life line! Throw out the life line!
Someone is sinking today.

Jesus is able! To you who are driven,
Farther and farther from God and from Heaven,
Helpless and hopeless, o'erwhelmed by the wave,
We throw out the life line, 'tis Jesus can save.

This is the life line, oh grasp it today.
See, you are recklessly drifting away,
Voices in warning, shout over the wave,
O grasp the strong life line, for Jesus can save.

As I ponder the great mysteries of God and how He intervenes in the hard circumstances of our lives, I know He has the answers to all of our life experiences. I know He brought this old song to my mind just now, in part, to remind me of how timeless His love is, and how unfathomable is the depth of His ability to save us from despair.

Forgiveness

There have been many opportunities for forgiveness during this struggle. We know we have battles ahead of us, but for now, we are striving to support Chandler in every way possible. I saved Chandler's last two paragraphs for this section. He sums it up pretty well…

"Mimi heard my cry for help. She started calling me Chandler and using the correct pronouns; I was tired of distancing myself from her. Though my heart had been torn and stretched in ways I cannot even begin to explain, I knew I needed to start letting her in again—I needed to meet her in the middle. So, my relationship with Mimi went slowly but surely back to what it was before. Yes, my brain still has times where it goes back to a bad habit and a part of me despises her, but my heart always wins.

At the end of the day, I love Mimi. Though I am simply not the person I was three years ago, I am so happy that I can start forming a "Mimi and Chandler" relationship. Yes, of course, I will remember what she said to me, just like she will remember what I said to her . . . but maybe that's not a bad thing? It has helped us and changed us. I would rather have a million bad days which led to a million good days afterward, than a life full of only bad days."

Forgiveness is one of the most cathartic decisions we make as humans. It takes both *humility of our spirit* and *relinquishment of our will* to look at ourselves the way others see us, and most importantly, the way God sees us. Though it is painful to let go of our stubborn will, the gift of peace is always worth the effort. God's peace … the peace that passes understanding.

67

The Dilemma

68

We Don't Know What We Don't Know

—BY SUSAN—

When watching *"The Shack"* the night I realized the Lord was speaking to me about learning new things (p.61), I became anxious. Up to that point, I was confused and frustrated on how to deal with Caroline, because I *thought* I knew exactly what *God's* position was concerning transgender people. I never imagined the Lord would turn this situation into a learning opportunity for *me*. Since it also hadn't occurred to me that our family would ever deal with transgender issues, the naive bubble in which I lived was bursting.

Some thoughts have come to me as I continue to meet with the Lord and ask Him to guide me through this maze of confusion. We Christians have long used the mantra "love the sinner, hate the sin." Most of us are very aware of our own sin. Because I desire this "love the sinner" response from others, I try to remember that in God's sight, sin is sin. It's not first degree, second degree, and third degree—it's all sin which He freely forgives when we ask with a repentant heart.

So, why then do we put a bright red "X" mark on transgenders, similar to the "A" worn by Hester Prynne in Nathaniel Hawthorne's *The Scarlet Letter?*

Is it our job to judge?

Matthew 7:1-5 (NIV)

[1]"Do not judge, or you too will be judged. [2]For in the same way you judge others, you will be judged, and with the measure you use, it will be measured to you. [3]Why do you look at the speck of sawdust in your brother's eye and pay no attention to the plank in your own eye? [4]How can you say to your brother, 'Let me take the speck out of your eye,' when all the time there is a plank in your own eye? [5]You hypocrite, first take the plank out of your own eye, and then you will see clearly to remove the speck from your brother's eye."

I was also reminded of a scientific discovery. Do you remember when Klinefelter Syndrome was big news? Named after Dr. Harry Klinefelter in 1942, the features that came to be recognized as Klinefelter's syndrome focused primarily on the onset of some traditionally female symptoms in males (including breast growth). In the late 1950's, however, the syndrome was expanded by identification of one or more extra X chromosomes in some males. Below is a portion of the article published by Mayo Clinic:

> [2]Klinefelter Syndrome is a genetic condition that results when a boy is born with an extra copy of the X chromosome. Klinefelter Syndrome is a common genetic condition affecting males, and it often isn't diagnosed until adulthood.
>
> Klinefelter Syndrome may adversely affect testicular growth, resulting in smaller than normal testicles, which can lead to lower production of testosterone. The syndrome may also cause reduced muscle mass, reduced body and facial hair, and enlarged breast tissue. The effects of Klinefelter Syndrome vary, and not everyone has the same signs and symptoms.

My thought is that this abnormality might have been around for thousands of years, but was not described until 1942. With the many scientific discoveries made over the last century, it is possible that many unknowns concerning transgender children are yet to be discovered through scientific study of the mind and brain.

---

[2] Mayo Clinic article published October 4, 2016

What We Do Know

—BY SUSAN—

When we come to the place where we realize our child is at risk, the next step is to find out all we can about the issue. Ashlea was helpful in patiently discussing the fine points of the transgender world, and how Chandler fit into the patterns. It was overwhelming! When the word "suicide" came up, we knew we had to become proactive.

Several scientific transgender studies came to my attention during my research. With the unparalleled level of transgender suicide attempts, scientists have already determined through the autopsy of those who succeeded, that there were marked differences in both the size and physical appearance of transgender brains. Here are their findings:

[3]Transgender Study Looks at 'Exceptionally High' Suicide-Attempt Rate

A whopping 41% of people who are transgender or gender-nonconforming have attempted suicide sometime in their lives, nearly nine times the national average, according to a sweeping survey released in 2011. *The rate has steadily risen to 57% since that article was written in 2011.*

In a newer study released in January 2014, researchers dug deeper into that number, analyzing the results of the National Transgender Discrimination Survey to examine what puts transgender people at such "exceptionally high" risk.

Researchers from the American Foundation for Suicide Prevention and the Williams Institute at UCLA School of Law found that the risk of attempting suicide was especially severe for transgender or gender-nonconforming people who had suffered discrimination or violence, such as being physically or sexually assaulted at work or school.

---

[3] January 28, 2014|By Emily Alpert Reyes

Susan Butler

[4]Is There Something Unique about the Transgender Brain?

Imaging Studies and Other Research Suggest That There Is a Biological Basis for Transgender Identity

Some children insist, from the moment they can speak, that they are not the gender indicated by their biological sex. So, where does this knowledge reside? And is it possible to discern a genetic or anatomical basis for transgender identity? Exploration of these questions is relatively new, but there is a bit of evidence for a genetic basis. Identical twins are somewhat more likely than fraternal twins to both be trans.

Male and female brains are, on average, slightly different in structure, although there is tremendous individual variability. Several studies have looked for signs that transgender people have brains more similar to their experienced gender. Spanish investigators—led by psychobiologist Antonio Guillamon of the National Distance Education University in Madrid and neuropsychologist Carme Junqu Plaja of the University of Barcelona—used MRI scans to examine the brains of 24 female-to-males and 18 male-to-females—both before and after treatment with cross-sex hormones.

Their results, published in 2013, showed that even before treatment the brain structures of the trans people were more similar in some respects to the brains of their experienced gender than those of their natal gender. For example, the female-to-male subjects had relatively thin subcortical areas (these areas tend to be thinner in men than in women). Male-to-female subjects tended to have thinner cortical regions in the right hemisphere, which is characteristic of a female brain. (Such differences became more pronounced after treatment.)

"Trans people have brains that are different from males and females, a unique kind of brain," Guillamon says. "It is simplistic to say that a female-to-male transgender person is a female trapped in a male

---

[4] By Francine Russo, a veteran journalist, specializing in psychology and behavior, January 1, 2016.

72

body [sic]. It's not because they have a male brain but a transsexual brain [sic]." Of course, behavior and experience shape brain anatomy, so it is impossible to say if these subtle differences are inborn.

Other investigators have looked at sex differences through brain functioning. In a study published in 2014, psychologist Sarah M. Burke of VU University Medical Center in Amsterdam and biologist Julie Bakker of the Netherlands Institute for Neuroscience used functional MRI to examine how 39 pre-pubertal and 41 adolescent boys and girls with gender dysphoria responded to androstadienone, an odorous steroid with pheromone-like properties that is known to cause a different response in the hypothalamus of men versus women. They found that the adolescent boys and girls with gender dysphoria responded much like peers of their experienced gender. The results were less clear with the prepubertal children.

This kind of study is important, says Baudewijntje Kreukels, an expert on gender dysphoria at VU University Medical Center, "because sex differences in responding to odors cannot be influenced by training or environment." The same can be said of another 2014 experiment by Burke and her colleagues. They measured the responses of boys and girls with gender dysphoria to echolike sounds produced by the inner ear in response to a clicking noise. Boys with gender dysphoria responded more like typical females, who have a stronger response to these sounds. But girls with gender dysphoria also responded like typical females.

Overall, the weight of these studies and others points strongly toward a biological basis for gender dysphoria. But given the variety of transgender people and the variation in the brains of men and women generally, it will be a long time, if ever, before a doctor can do a brain scan on a child and say, "Yes, this child is trans."

Susan Butler

[5]Born This Way?

Researchers Explore the Science of Gender Identity

A consortium of five research institutions in Europe and the United States, including Vanderbilt University Medical Center, George Washington University, and Boston Children's Hospital, is looking to the *genome*, a person's complete set of DNA, for clues about whether transgender people are born this way. Two decades of brain research have provided hints of a biological origin to being transgender, but no irrefutable conclusions.

Now scientists in the consortium have embarked on what they call the largest-ever study of its kind, searching for a genetic component to explain why people assigned one gender at birth so persistently identify as the other, often from very <u>early childhood</u>.

Researchers have extracted DNA from the blood samples of 10,000 people, 3,000 of them transgender and the rest non-transgender, or cisgender. The project is awaiting grant funding to begin the next phase: testing about 3 million markers, or variations, across the *genome* for all of the samples.

UPDATE: The DNA research on 10,000 people (above paragraph) is currently underway. The new research is published in the *<u>Journal of Clinical Endocrinology & Metabolism</u>*.

---

[5] *U.S. News* <u>August 4, 2017</u> by Daniel Trotta

[6]Scans Show Difference in Transgender Brains

A team of scientists has discovered differences in the brains of transgender people.

The researchers, at the National University of Distance Education in Madrid, Spain, believe their technique could help doctors identify transgender people at an early age, giving them more options for treatment, such as delaying the onset of puberty.

According to *New Scientist*, the study looked at the white matter of the brain and its structural differences in men, women, and female-to-male transgender people.

They used MRI scans on the brains of 18 trans men who had not started hormone treatment with 24 men and 19 women [sic].

The results showed that trans men – those born biologically female but living as male – had white matter where it is usually found in male brains.

This is thought to be the first time that scientists have been able to show that trans men's brains are masculinized.

In another study, they compared the brains of 18 trans women – born male but living as female – with 19 men and 19 women [sic].

The trans women's brains showed that the structure of the white matter was halfway between a typical male and a typical female brain.

Antonio Guillamon, who led the research, said: "Their brains are not completely masculinized and not completely feminized, but they still feel female." The study will be published in Volume 45, Issue 2 of the Journal of Psychiatric Research in September 2017.

---

[6] Pink News-Health, <u>August 2017</u>

[7]Interview with Nathan Grant Smith, Ph. D.

Dr. Nathan Grant Smith is an Associate Professor in the Department of Psychological, Health, and Learning Sciences in the College of Education at the University of Houston. His main area of research focuses on stress and coping, with emphases on lesbian, gay, bisexual, and transgender persons and persons living with or at risk of contracting HIV. Currently, his research focuses on the intersection of minority stress and health behaviors among lesbian, gay, bisexual, and transgender persons.

Professional Biography

Dr. Smith's research has been funded by the National Institutes of Health and the Canadian Institutes of Health Research. He is a Fellow of the American Psychological Association (APA) and of APA's Division 17 (Society of Counseling Psychology) and Division 44 (Society for the Psychological Study of Lesbian, Gay, Bisexual, and Transgender Issues). In addition, he is a recipient of the APA Division 17 Section for Lesbian, Gay, Bisexual, and Transgender Issues Award for Significant Contribution to Social Justice and Advocacy. He is a licensed psychologist in the state of Texas.

Dr. Smith received his Bachelor of Arts at Southern Methodist University in Dallas, TX, and his Master of Science and Doctor of Philosophy, both in Counseling Psychology, at Virginia Commonwealth University in Richmond, VA. He completed a predoctoral internship at the University of Maryland Counseling Center in College Park, MD, and a postdoctoral fellowship in HIV prevention research at the Center for

---

[7] Associate Professor of Counseling Psychology in the Department of Psychological, Health, and Learning Sciences in the College of Education at the University of Houston, Houston, Texas.

Interdisciplinary Research on AIDS (CIRA) at the Yale University School of Medicine in New Haven, CT.

After completing his research training, Dr. Smith completed a Congressional fellowship through the American Association for the Advancement of Science and the American Psychological Association. During his fellowship, he served as a legislative fellow in the United States Senate Committee on Health, Education, Labor, and Pensions under Senator Edward M. Kennedy. Dr. Smith's policy portfolio included HIV/AIDS, mental health, and substance abuse.

Dr. Smith served as an assistant professor for four years in the Department of Psychology and Philosophy at Texas Woman's University in Denton, TX. He then served on the faculty of the Department of Educational and Counselling Psychology at McGill University, Montreal, QC, where he was awarded tenure and promotion to Associate Professor. After five years at McGill, he joined the Department of Psychological, Health, and Learning Sciences at the University of Houston. He is currently an Associate Professor in the Department.

Q & A with Dr. Nathan G. Smith

Q1 What percentage of your research is related to transgender issues?

Approximately 80% of my research focuses on transgender issues.

Q2 Over the course of your research, approximately how much of your time has been devoted to those who identify as transgender, and what is the age span of these individuals?

Most of my research has been inclusive of transgender persons. Indeed, most of my research samples include transgender participants who also identify as lesbian, gay, bisexual, or queer. Together with one of my doctoral students at McGill University, I have published two articles* focused on transgender resilience against suicidality.

It's hard to quantify how much of my time is devoted to transgender individuals—I continually strive to be mindful of the issues facing transgender persons in my research and to be inclusive of a range of gender identities in my research. My focus is on adults, aged 18 and over. I have done a good amount of research on young adults but do not focus on children or adolescents in my own work.

Q3 Can you share the latest medical research on transgender persons?

As a psychologist, my focus is more on behavioral issues facing transgender adults. However, I am well-versed in the general scientific literature examining the lives of transgender persons. In general, gender identity is a relatively enduring and fundamental part of the human experience. Transgender people have existed throughout time, across cultures, and on every inhabited continent. However, colonization resulted in the suppression and marginalization of trans identities. Examples include Native American two-spirit identities, in which two-spirit individuals often have had important leadership roles within the community. In South Asian cultures, hijras are regarded as sacred.

Gender identity should be understood as related to but distinct from sexual orientation. Gender identity refers to a person's deeply felt internal sense of self as male, female, neither, both, or an alternative gender. Sexual orientation, on the other hand, refers to the gender or genders to whom one is romantically, emotionally, and/or sexually attracted. While numerically there are more people who are cisgender (i.e., their gender matches the gender they were assigned at birth) and heterosexual (i.e., attracted to those with a different gender), millions of people in the US alone identify as transgender, with a recent study suggesting that 1.4 million people in the US identify as transgender.

Some transgender individuals may seek medical transition-related care, such as using hormones or gender-affirmative surgeries (such as chest masculinization, vaginoplasty, or hysterectomy), while other individuals may not. For many transgender individuals, being able to transition (be that medically, socially, or otherwise) is a positive and protective factor in their lives. Indeed, in research I conducted with my student Chérie Moody, we found that the hope of transitioning, as well as actually transitioning, was viewed as life-saving. Transgender adult research participants told us that transitioning or the hope of transitioning was one of the things that kept them from acting on their suicidal thoughts.

Related to the point above, transgender individuals face a number of health disparities that put them at risk for illness and death. These disparities—in things like suicide, smoking, substance use, homelessness, poverty, and mental health problems—are strongly linked to the pervasive stigma, discrimination, and prejudice they experience. In regards to suicide attempts, rates in the general US population are around 2-9%, whereas rates of suicide attempts among transgender individuals have been found to be as high as 41%. As I note above, we also see higher rates of a variety of health problems. For example, 35.5% of transgender adults smoke cigarettes versus 14.9% of the general population. It's not hard to understand why transgender individuals are at risk of a variety of negative health outcomes. The transgender community faces bullying, family rejection, violence, lack of access to health care and education, and discrimination in housing and employment.

While it's true that there are a number of risks for transgender people— resulting from the stigma and discrimination they experience— it's important to note that transgender people are incredibly resilient. Transgender people not only survive these challenges but they thrive. They create connections with others, create communities, look out for each other, and contribute immensely to our world.

It's also important to note that transgender people are the experts on their own lives. There is no one way to be trans. Being trans is not a passing fad. Whereas for some people gender may be fluid, for most trans people, their gender identity is a stable, enduring, and important part of who they are (just like it is for most cis people). In addition, there is nothing inherently pathological about being transgender. The vast majority of problems facing trans people are a result of the unsupportive environments they are in—not because of anything inherent in being trans. Indeed, the World Health Organization recently announced that they would be moving "gender incongruence" from the *mental disorder section* to the *sexual health section* of the International Classification of Diseases catalog.

Q4 What would you say are the most challenging problems transgender persons deal with?

As I note above, the biggest issues are usually related to stigma and discrimination. Being rejected because of who they are can be extremely painful. But having supportive families, friends, faith communities, and other communities are incredibly powerful. We all need love and acceptance, especially when there are forces out there telling you that you are less-than. In addition, transgender people face the same struggles we all face: workplace stress, relationship stress, financial stress.

Q5 What needs seem to be universal within the trans community?

Trans individuals—just like all of us—want to *exercise their own agency*. To be autonomous, make their own decisions, and be supported by others. Respect goes a long way. Trans people know themselves.

Respecting their pronouns, respecting their names, respecting their basic humanity is crucial. Unfortunately, too often that respect is lacking.

Q6 What advice would you give to the families of trans children?

In general, the research shows that gender expansive behavior early in childhood (preschool and early elementary) may or may not persist. For some children, that may later translate to a trans identity but for others it won't. People may come out as transgender during childhood, adolescence, or adulthood. For many adults, they have usually hidden this part of themselves from others (and in some cases, tried to hide it from themselves) for years. Regardless of when children come out—or even if they display behavior that is not normative for their sex assigned at birth—parental support is the best policy. Given how much stigma there is in society, providing a supportive and accepting atmosphere can go a long way in helping trans children. In my own research with Chérie Moody, family support emerged as one of the most important protective factors against suicide. The World Health Organization proclaims: "Suicide is a serious, preventable global health problem."

Parents should educate themselves about transgender issues and talk to their children about how they can be supportive. There are many resources available for parents including:

Gender Spectrum (https://www.genderspectrum.org)
Gender Diversity (http://www.genderdiversity.org)
PFLAG (http://www.pflag.org)
TransYouth Family Allies (http://www.imatyfa.org)
Gender Infinity (http://genderinfinity.org)
Human Rights Campaign's transgender children and youth resource page (http://www.hrc.org/explore/topic/transgender-children-youth).

*Articles mentioned in "Q6" above are listed below:

1.   **Suicide Protective Factors Among Trans Adults,** McGill University, Department of Educational and Counseling Psychology, Montreal, Canada. Arch Sex Behav (2013) 42:739-752, DOI

10:1007/s10508-013-0099-8. Authors: Dr. Nathan G. Smith and his doctoral student Cherie Moody

    2.   **"Without This, I Would for Sure Already Be Dead":** A Qualitative Inquiry Regarding Suicide Protective Factors Among Trans Adults, Psychology of Sexual Orientation & Gender Diversity 2015, Vol. 2, No. 3, 266-280, American Psychological Association, 2329-0382/15/$12.00.   http://dx.doi.org/10.1037/sgd0000130.   Authors: Cherie Moody, McGill University, Nate Fuks, The Argyle Institute of Human Relations, Sandra Pelaez, McGill University, Nathan Grant Smith, University of Houston.

[8]A Come to Jesus Talk on Transgender Youth

"Knowing all of this, who would decide that a 57% youth suicide attempt rate is an acceptable risk, based only on a scriptural gray area? What sort of person would decide the chance to bury a child in 'gender appropriate' clothing is worth the cost? Have they ever asked someone what it's like to <u>lose a Transgender child</u> because you couldn't accept them?"

The above statement is an excerpt of an opinion piece written by Brynn Tannehill. The language is strong, indeed a bit harsh; the "gray area" premise debatable. Yet, the sobering truth is that none of us wants to lose our child because we chose judgment over love—

1 CORINTHIANS 13:13 (NIV)

"AND NOW THESE THREE REMAIN:

FAITH, HOPE AND LOVE.

BUT THE GREATEST OF THESE IS LOVE."

---

[8] Brynn Tannehill, Blogger, <u>November 4, 2014</u>

The Trevor Project

The Trevor Project is the leading and only accredited national organization providing crisis intervention and suicide prevention services to lesbian, gay, bisexual, transgender, queer, and questioning young people under the age of 25.

The Trevor Project offers a suite of crisis intervention and suicide prevention programs, including TrevorLifeline, TrevorText, and TrevorChat as well as a peer-to-peer social network support for transgender young people under the age of 25, TrevorSpace.

Trevor also offers an education program with resources for youth-serving adults and organizations, a legislative advocacy department fighting for pro-transgender legislation and against anti-transgender rhetoric/policy positions, and conducts research to discover the most effective means to help young transgender people in crisis and end suicide.

If you or someone you know is feeling hopeless or suicidal, the Trevor Lifeline crisis counselors are available 24/7/365 at 866.488.7386.

www.TheTrevorProject.org

The Genecis Program
Children's Health Specialty Center at Dallas[9]

The GENECIS Program at Children's Health focuses on helping children and teens with issues surrounding gender dysphoria—the distress that may occur when an individual does not identify with the gender they were assigned at birth. Gender dysphoria is frequently associated with mental health conditions such as depression, anxiety, and a very elevated suicide attempt rate at 41 percent. Gender dysphoria also causes clinically significant distress or impairment in social, occupational, or other important areas of functioning.

The GENECIS Program recognizes the need for comprehensive care including prescribing puberty blockers and hormone replacement therapy when appropriate, to gender non-conforming adolescents. This is recognized as Standard of Care treatment by the Endocrine Society Guidelines for the medical care of transgender adolescents.

The program is heavily rooted in mental health support. The GENECIS team works closely with a number of specialists in psychology, psychiatry, endocrinology, adolescent medicine, gynecology, social work, pastoral care and ethics, to determine the best route for patient care and to provide information and support to meet the medical and emotional needs of patients and their family. What is the GENECIS Protocol and Evaluation Process?

In order to be a patient in the GENECIS program, one of our social workers will perform a phone intake to determine what your concerns are and to help us know if your child meets the requirements to be a patient in our program.

---

[9] Children's Health GENECIS Program, copied from their website: www.childrens.com, 9/1/2017

These requirements include:

1) Age 4-17.
2) Have an established mental health provider (therapist), if your child does not have one, we will provide the necessary resources.
3) A letter from your child's therapist supporting the diagnosis of gender dysphoria.

Once your child meets these criteria, an assessment by mental health providers will be scheduled. This assessment is a face to face, four-hour meeting with both parents or legal guardians (whenever possible) and your child.

Subsequently, your child's case will be discussed with our multidisciplinary team to evaluate recommendations regarding starting puberty suppression therapy (puberty blockers), hormone replacement therapy, as well as mental health and social needs. Gender affirming surgery is *not* performed at Children's Health.

With a suicide attempt rate of up to 60 percent for youth with gender dysphoria, the GENECIS Program recognizes the need for comprehensive care including prescribing puberty blockers, when appropriate, to gender nonconforming adolescents. Prescribing puberty blockers is a standard of care that grants time to gender dysphoric adolescents as they contemplate their long-term gender identity.

89

The Challenge

90

What Would Jesus Do?

—BY SUSAN—

What *would* Jesus Do? I'm neither scholar nor theologian, and like many of us mere mortals, I don't even like to think about the answers to some of today's social issues. As I mentioned in the Prologue, we seek to understand that which affects us most personally. So, if we aren't personally affected by a transgender person, we just might not think too deeply about it. And, if we are associated with one who identifies as transgender, we might be afraid to find out what God's Word says.

What if you *are* affected by a person under the trans umbrella? Do you have a relative who has embraced it in one way or another, or maybe your child is friends with a trans person? What if your child has been reading all of the easily accessible transgender information, and has decided he is transgender? What if you have become confused and frustrated by a world that labels you a homophobe for disagreeing with the trans identity which may include same-sex attraction, when you have been taught all your life that same-sex love is a sin?

As a trans person, what if you have been treated like a second-class citizen and been bullied because of your transition? What if you were miserable trying to fit in as a heterosexual teen, but found that you became complete when you identified as trans? What if your parents and other family members have abandoned you because of your transgender status? What if you embraced the trans life, but lost your desire to practice your faith in the process?

Do you really want to know what Jesus would do?
    I believe He would love them.
    I believe He would draw them to Himself.
    I believe He would teach them.
    I believe He would ask them to trust Him with their lives,
    just like He asks all of us to do.

Susan Butler

Conclusions from Scripture
—BY SUSAN—

It's now time to look for answers to these questions. Together, let us search for Truth. And where better to find Truth than from the One who

Knows it All — Made it All — Loves us All — Forgives us All

Q1 What does God think about you, the individual He created?

Psalm 139:13-16 (NASB)

13 For you formed my inward parts; you wove me in my mother's womb. 14 I will give thanks to you, for I am fearfully and wonderfully made; wonderful are your works, and my soul knows it very well. 15 My frame was not hidden from you, when I was made in secret, and skillfully wrought in the depths of the earth; 16 your eyes have seen my unformed substance; and in your Book were all written the days that were ordained for me, when as yet there was not one of them.

World View: Though the majority of Americans still believe in God, there is much disagreement about Creation and when Life begins.

God's View: *You are one-of-a-kind.* God made you with an exclusive DNA and fingerprints. No one is just like you. With the billions of souls who have lived and died, you are distinctly different. Before He made you, He knew exactly how long your life would be, and knows even the number of hairs on your head. God doesn't love you because you are valuable—*you are valuable because God loves you.*

Q2 Will we have an excuse if we choose to ignore God?

Romans 1:20-22:(NASB)

[20]For since the creation of the world His invisible attributes, His eternal power and divine nature, have been clearly seen, being understood through what has been made, so that they are without excuse. [21]For even though they knew God, they did not honor Him as God, or give thanks, but they became futile in their speculations, and their foolish heart was darkened. [22]Professing to be wise, they became fools.

World View: The world suggests that you can pick and choose the parts of the Bible that fit your opinion and lifestyle; that believing all of God's Word is foolish.

God's View: God's Word says that believing that lie is the very essence of becoming a fool, and those who do not believe in Him are without excuse.

Q3 Is the Word of God obsolete?

Hebrews 4:12-13

[12]For the word of god is living and active, and sharper than any two-edged sword, piercing as far as the division of soul and spirit, of both joints and marrow, and able to judge the thoughts and intentions of the heart. [13]and there is no creature hidden from his sight, but all things are open and laid bare to the eyes of him with whom we have to do.

World View: It is tempting to believe the writers of the Bible could not possibly understand today's problems—the sexual revolution, wars, immigration, murder, suicide, fraud in both politics and religion … need I go on? History refutes that idea with numerous accounts from the beginning of time on every issue just listed here. It may be somewhat easier to hide our sins from the world; but, even our best attempts to hide our imperfect lives can be thwarted with the loud voice of social media.

God's View: Because God knows our hearts, neither our thoughts nor our intentions can be hidden from Him. As our Creator, He understands us better than we understand ourselves, and therefore has the ability to engage us with His wisdom when we seek Him. God's Word obsolete? It has never been more relevant than it is today.

Q4 How does God love us?

John 3:16,17 (NASB)

16For God so loved the world (every individual past, present and future) that He gave His only begotten Son (Jesus), that whoever believes in Him shall not perish, but have eternal life. 17For God did not send the Son into the world to judge the world, but that the world might be saved through Him.

World View: Some consider that there are many legitimate Gods based on one's own religion; that it doesn't matter which God you worship. They think that believing *Jesus is the one and only Savior* is an affront to all other religions.

God's View: While other faiths pray to their god, if you search history you will find that no other god died for the sins of mankind and subsequently rose from the grave to prepare a place for all who choose to follow Him. There is no other deity with whom you can have a personal relationship—a Friend—as scripture describes below:

John 15:13 (NIV)

Greater love hath no one than this: to lay down one's life for one's friends.

The context of this scripture points to Jesus as that friend. There exists no more noble and consequential sacrifice than Jesus Christ's act of perfect love.

Q5 Why did Jesus die for us?

John 12:46-47 (NASB)

46"I have come as light into the world, that everyone who believes in Me may not remain in darkness. 47And if anyone hears My sayings, and does not keep them, I do not judge him; for I did not come to judge the world, but to save the world."

World View: Most people have the misconception that Jesus came to judge us. The scriptures are very clear that The Law of the Old Testament was replaced by Christ's Law of Grace in the New Testament. Until Christ came, blood and grain sacrifices were made using animals and crops, and over 600 rules had to be followed.

God's View: Jesus said: "I did not come to judge the world, but to save it." God loves us equally. He sacrificed His Son for each one of us. Why did He do this? Not because we deserve it or because we have been more obedient than others. He did it to save each of us from our sinful selves and offer us the free gift of eternal life. All we have to do is tell Him we accept and receive His Gift of salvation, then follow Him.

Q6 What was God's plan for creating Adam and Eve?

Genesis 1:26-28 (NASB)

[26]Then God said, "Let us make man in Our image, according to Our likeness; and let them rule over the fish of the sea and over the birds of the sky and over the cattle and over all the earth and over every creeping thing that creeps on the earth." [27]And God created man in His own image, in the image of God He created him; male and female He created them. [28]God blessed them; and God said to them, "Be fruitful and multiply, and fill the earth, and subdue it"

World View: It seems the world chooses to question the story of Creation as it relates to God's creation of male and female in His own image. They ask, "If God made us all in His image, why do some of us feel so strongly about our sexual orientation being different from others of our sex?" This applies to same-sex attraction, but also to transgender persons where the question is not so much their sexual attractions, but their gender identity. Trans persons also deal with *dysphoria* which causes them to detest the body they were given at birth, thus creating another dilemma as they question why God made them one gender, yet they feel strongly that they are the opposite gender.

The questions are legitimate and honest. How do non-heterosexual individuals exist and survive the judgment of others in an overwhelmingly heterosexual world?

God's View: After making everything in heaven and earth, God made Adam and Eve in His own perfect image. He made both male and female in order to fulfill the roles of His plan for us to multiply and fill the earth and subdue it. His plan began with one woman and one man, and His purpose was for them to multiply His creation.

Even in this first family union, however, the children born to Adam and Eve were notably *imperfect*. Their parents exercised their God-given free will and participated in eating of the forbidden fruit of the "tree of knowledge of good evil." This act is commonly referred to as "original sin," and changed the course of human history.

God made each of us uniquely different with various talents and temperaments. As we explore those traits that make each of us individuals, we find ourselves drawn to certain types of people. It is evident in scripture that though God created us, we have all been born into an imperfect world where no one achieves perfection.

When we stand before God, one of the great questions of our time may be, "Why, God, were some of us born different?" Our responsibility until then is to allow God to speak to each of us, accepting that He loves each of us the same, but deals with each of us differently.

For example, we deal with members of our family individually because of their different strengths and weaknesses. In much the same way, because God knows our innermost thoughts, He deals with an alcoholic in ways that suit the alcoholic's needs, and the habitual liar in ways that suit his needs. We human beings do not have the capacity within ourselves to "get it right" every time, but we have access to the One who can teach us how.

Q7 The passage below concerns *God's judgment*, and *His condemnation* of those who sit in judgment of sinners when they are guilty themselves.
How does this apply to our question of God's will for us to accept those whose sins are different from—or in our minds condemned "worse than"—ours?

John 8:3-11 (NIV)

³The teachers of the law and the Pharisees brought in a woman caught in adultery. They made her stand before the group and said to Jesus, ⁴"Teacher, this woman was caught in the act of adultery. ⁵In the Law Moses commanded us to stone such women. Now what do you say?" ⁶They were using this question as a trap, in order to have a basis for accusing

him. But Jesus bent down and started to write on the ground with his finger. [7]When they kept on questioning him, he straightened up and said to them, "Let any one of you who is without sin be the first to throw a stone at her." [8]Again, he stooped down and wrote on the ground. [9]At this, those who heard began to go away one at a time, the older ones first, until only Jesus was left, with the woman still standing there. [10]Jesus straightened up and asked her, "Woman, where are they? Has no one condemned you?" [10]"No one, sir," she said. "Then neither do I condemn you." Jesus declared. "Go now and leave your life of sin."

World View: Have you noticed a trend in today's world about judgment? There is a paradoxical shift in thinking by those who are offended by anyone who disagrees with their view on a given subject. They are quick to yell "don't judge," but are doing the same thing as they vent their animus concerning the opposing viewpoint. Particularly when morality, religion, or politics emerge in conversation or through the media, any sense of judgment from one side evokes extreme retaliation from the other side. I think Jesus was on to something as He shifted the focus of the Pharisees from the sin of the adulteress to the sin of the men threatening her life.

God's View: In this passage, the sin of adultery is committed by a woman and several men. But only the woman is being threatened and judged, not the men in her life. The sin of judging this woman is committed by a group of male teachers, and Jesus makes it painfully clear that judgment of another's sin is a sin itself. The parable points to Jesus as One who knows us, has compassion for us, and freely forgives us. His forgiveness leads us to repentance, and because we are not yet perfected, we will continue to sin. Therefore, no one is free to judge another's sin.

Q8 How do we show God's love to those we disagree with; to those whose lifestyle choices are different from ours?

1 John 4:11-12 (NIV)

[11] Dear friends, since God so loved us, we also ought to love one another. [12]No one has ever seen God; but if we love one another, God lives in us and his love is made complete in us.

World View: We all deserve to be loved, the world tells us, no matter what we do. The interesting thing about that concept is that as human beings, we tend to show conditional love to those with whom we disagree. If they act, speak, love, give, etc., in a way that is different from our view of normal, we may withhold love and acceptance. Our love has conditions.

God's View: God's love, on the other hand, is unconditional. We show God's love, Agape Love, by loving one another unconditionally. To accomplish this, we look past the faults of our co-workers, neighbors, friends, family and even strangers—toward the One who made us. God's love in us will propel us to love others with the same love with which He loves us.

Q9 Jesus said the entire Law and the Prophets depend upon what two commandments?

Matthew 22:35-40 (NIV)

35One of them, an expert in the law, tested Him with this question, 36"Teacher, which is the greatest commandment in the Law?" 37Jesus replied, "Love the Lord your God with all your heart, and with all your soul, and with all your mind." 38This is the first and greatest commandment. 39And the second is like it: "Love your neighbor as yourself." 40All the Law and the Prophets hang on these two commandments."

World View: The world tries to manipulate what is most important. Some say we have the right to be happy. Some say we have the right to be free. These are both good ideals to which most subscribe. But other opinions of our rights are far less noble, such as believing we have the right to live in whatever manner we desire. Still others say they have the right to choose what they do with their bodies. Yet, none of these are *rights*. Some are blessings. Others are self-inflicted wounds that may carry with them years of physical and mental degradation.

God's View: Jesus said **loving the Lord our God** and **loving others as ourselves** are the two commandments upon which the Law and the Prophets *depend.* If that is so, then <u>Love triumphs over the Law and Prophets of the Old Testament</u>. He is testifying that no other commandment nor prophecy has the *priority* of loving God and loving each other. This is an extraordinary pronouncement of Truth we can depend on—because it is spoken by the Son of God!

Q10 What does the Bible say about The Law in the Old Testament vs Grace in the New Testament? How does this principle apply to our transgender friends and family? Should trans persons be loved and accepted in our communities and houses of worship?

Romans 5:20-21 (NIV)

[20]The law was brought in so that the trespass might increase. But where sin increased, grace increased all the more, [21]so that, just as sin reigned in death, so also grace might reign through righteousness to bring eternal life through Jesus Christ our Lord.

Romans 6:14 (NIV)

For sin shall no longer be your master, because you are not under the law, but under grace.

World View: The world likes the idea of a God of Grace. Why not? Since we aren't under the Law anymore, can we just keep on enjoying our sinful habits? Well, not really … because our sins separate us from God.

God's View: This passage applies to all of us who were under the Law until we found the free gift of God's grace through faith in Jesus Christ. He came to love us and save us—not to condemn us. Neither should we, then, condemn those who live differently or believe differently, but grace them with God's love. We are under grace—God's Riches at Christ's Expense—we must give this grace to others.

Q11 What can we do to promote family unity and love when we have children who are expressing dissatisfaction with their gender and hatred for their body?

Psalm 127:3a (NIV)
Children are a heritage from the Lord.

Proverbs 12:18 (NIV)
The words of the reckless pierce like swords, but the tongue of the wise brings healing.

Proverbs 22:6 (NASB)
Train up a child in the way he should go, and even when he is old, he will not depart from it.

Luke 17:2 (NIV)

It would be better for them to be thrown into the sea with a millstone tied around their neck than to cause one of these little ones to stumble.

Colossians 3:21(NASB)
Fathers, do not exasperate your children, so that they will not lose heart.

1 John 3:7 (NIV)
Dear children, do not let anyone lead you astray. The one who does what is right is righteous, just as He is righteous.

1 John 5:2 (NIV)
This is how we know that we love the children of God: by loving God and carrying out His commands.

World View: The world tempts us to spoil our children by giving in to every desire they have. We can get swept away by the things of the world, and the pressure to be the coolest parent. We give and coddle, sometimes realizing too late that saying "no" would have been the better gift. Admittedly, it takes energy and determination to discipline, so we sometimes use excuses to let them get away with disobedience and disrespect.

God's View: When our children are born, it is apparent that we have been given a special gift, a miracle. But, as they grow and reveal their sin nature (which sometimes seems as though we are looking at our own reflection), we finally realize that these children need a healthy balance of love and discipline. From the few verses above, we must apply the principles of wisdom and understanding, using compassion and love. We must invest ourselves in their lives, not just with money but with our time. They must feel secure in our love through discipline and achievable, realistic expectations. We must build their character, showing through our own actions, that honesty and integrity are to be desired.

And how do we accomplish all of these noble pursuits? If we agree that parental love strikes a balance between affection and discipline, expectations and acceptance, and grace in times of need, then we can ascribe to the last verse above— "we love the children of God by loving God and carrying out His commands."

The Love Chapter
The Message Translation

If I speak with human eloquence and angelic ecstasy but don't love, I'm nothing but the creaking of a rusty gate.

If I speak God's Word with power, revealing all his mysteries and making everything plain as day, and if I have faith that says to a mountain, "Jump," and it jumps, but I don't have love, I'm nothing.

If I give everything I won to the poor and even go to the stake to be burned as a martyr, but I don't love, I've gotten nowhere. So, no matter what I say, what I believe, and what I do, I'm bankrupt without love.

Love never gives up,

Love cares more for others than for self.

Love doesn't want what it doesn't have.

Love doesn't strut.

Doesn't have a swelled head,

Doesn't force itself on others,

Isn't always "me first,"

Doesn't fly off the handle,

Doesn't keep score of the sins of others,

Doesn't revel when others grovel,

Takes pleasure in the flowering of truth,

Puts up with anything,

Trusts God always,

Always looks for the best,

Never looks back,

But keeps going to the end.

Love never dies. Inspired speech will be over some day; praying in tongues will end; understanding will reach its limit. We know only a portion of the truth, and what we say about God is always incomplete. But when the Complete arrives, our incompletes will be canceled.

When I was an infant at my mother's breast, I gurgled and cooed like any infant. When I grew up, I left those infant ways for good.

We don't yet see things clearly. We're squinting in a fog, peering through a mist. But it won't be long before the weather clears and the sun shines bright! We'll see it all then, see it all as clearly as God sees us, knowing him directly just as he knows us!

But for right now, until that completeness, we have three things to do to lead us toward that consummation: Trust steadily in God, hope unswervingly, love extravagantly.

And the best of these three is love.

Susan Butler

Transparent

——BY ASHLEA——

Wife. Mom. Widow. Trans Parent. Advocate. I've been known by many names over the course of my adulthood, but let's start with Graduate. Since graduating from college in 1998, each season of my life has wrested more and more questions about who I am. One of my post-collegiate fantasies was to meet a kind, funny man with whom I could build a marriage and forge a family. I met that man in 1999, and in 2000 I became Wife. Specifically, Nick's Wife. We were married in my parents' back yard, with tents and twinkle lights, and even a delicate smattering of rain on the patio dance floor. Nick had two young sons from his first marriage, so I also became Stepmom. The boys, Bryce and Nickalous, walked down the aisle as groomsmen, dapper in their tiny tuxedos. We sang karaoke, drank beer from a cold keg, and played with my brother's English Mastiff puppies. It was an incredible party.

The early years of our marriage brought hurdles and some tempestuous valleys. We fought for and won custody of Nick's boys, which increased my responsibility level tenfold, but also expanded my capacity for patience, love, and happiness. Nick and I started a commercial cleaning and maintenance business with my father, which expanded my understanding of misery, sleeplessness, and debt. The company was Nick's passion, however, and it fueled him and gave him a sense of purpose. He drove a garbage truck when I met him, so running a company was beyond what he dreamed possible.

My dream was to have a child. I'd finally found a man with whom that journey seemed feasible, and I was excited to see how our individual natures and looks would manifest in a baby of our own. Further fueling my fervor was the child I placed for adoption in 1996. I was 23 years old, I'd dropped out of community college, and I was working as a secretary for $24,000 a year. My parents were completely supportive, but the decision to adopt out was mine alone. I found a young couple who couldn't have children of their own, and their kindness and grace confirmed I was making the right decision. I have always felt very solid about the adoption. But after carrying, laboring, delivering, and then leaving him at the hospital, I prayed I would be blessed with another opportunity to parent.

That perfectly pink blessing arrived in 2003, and we named her Caroline Jordan. She was hilarious from her first breath. She had curly blonde hair, and huge rosy red lips. We bathed and potty trained her, we nurtured her lightning-quick brain, and we attempted to keep dresses on her (though she preferred tank tops "what showed [her] muscles"). Caroline was an easy child who slept comfortably in the pitch black, and who rejected the pacifier at every suggestion. She loved her big brothers and Elmo, and she adored her daddy. I was Mom, and our family was complete.

Life rolled busily along, as it is wont to do. We slowed down long enough to smell an occasional rose, but we worked hard with our business and even harder with our kids. The wicked pace of self-employment began to take a toll on Nick's health, and shortly after Caroline's fourth birthday, he was admitted to the hospital for observation of a sudden headache that would not desist. There were tests and medications and doctors, and ultimately, on the second day of his hospitalization, there was death. Nick was 34 years old when he died. My new name was Widow.

Nick was more force of nature than human being, and his loss filled every pore. I second-guessed every decision, and I questioned everything I thought I knew to be true. Bryce and Nickalous went to live with their mother, and I endeavored, with the constant help of my parents, to understand why God would take a father from his children. Twelve years have passed since that hot Sunday morning, and I still second guess my parenting. What would Nick do about a particular instance of teenage insolence? What would Nick think about our baby starting high school? How would Nick react if Caroline told him that she now wanted to be addressed as 'he'?

I became Trans Parent in April of 2016. We legally changed my child's name to Chandler, and he demands to be addressed with male pronouns. My strong 16-year old is physically transitioning, and he's now in the throes of a second puberty. His voice is deepening, and a faint mustache has appeared above those huge rosy lips. People constantly ask me, "What would Nick say about this transition to Chandler?" I know exactly what he'd say in his blustery way, and it gives me comfort: "You're transgender? Huh. Well that's great. Now go clean your room."

I have had many names since I was Graduate. I've experienced professional achievements, and I've learned I am capable of falling in love again. I find peace and pride in all of my many names, but my proudest accomplishment is Single Mom. I am now also called Advocate. People tend to fear that which they do not understand, and I desperately want people to understand Chandler. I want them to see past the forest of the word "transgender" and see the oak tree that is my son.

Susan Butler

Chandler—The New Me
—BY CHANDLER—

It has been almost two years since I started HRT (hormone replacement therapy). I have truly seen myself become the guy I always felt myself to be. I rarely get misgendered nowadays because in public and in social settings, I am seen as 100% Chandler—from my broad shoulders and deep voice to my chest and facial hair.

NEW RELATIONSHIPS

Mimi—My relationship with Mimi has returned to the normal relationship we had while I was growing up, if not better. That woman is one of my best friends and biggest fans. I don't know where I would be now if it weren't in part for her. She did a complete 180 that has made me so proud, I'm happy to share our relationship with my friends and new people that I meet.

Humbug—Since I last wrote about CJ, he has completely changed in ways we didn't know he was capable of. It took him awhile, but once whatever it was clicked, he has never misgendered me since. I am so utterly proud of that man, and I will say that for the rest of my life.

Mom—Of course, Mom and I are still the best of friends, just as we were when this book was just an idea. She is my whole world and my hero. She amazes me not only in her support for me, but in her newfound deep respect for the trans community she has continued to research and understand as time has passed.

Epilogue

We are three years into Phase Two of this transgender journey with Chandler. So many changes took place in 2017, 2018 and 2019 as Chandler now begins his junior year. After in-depth counseling, and medical testing performed by the endocrinologist at Children's Health, Chandler began hormone therapy October 26, 2017. On March 29, 2018, his name change from Caroline to Chandler Jordan Palladino was made official and legal (Chandler's 15th birthday was June 9, 2018).

The process of private and Genecis group counseling continues. We don't know what lies ahead. Fear is real. What if the challenges are too great for Chandler? What if he decides five years from now that this transition has not accomplished his expectations? When we asked the counselors and doctors these questions, their only response is to consider the alternative: *If we do nothing or forbid hormone therapy, we must remember the suicide attempt rate of those children who do not feel supported and accepted by their families.* We hope for the best outcome. We pray for Chan to feel whole. Our goal is to support him in the good times and the bad, trusting that God has His hand on Chandler.

John 9 (NIV) tells the Parable of the Blind Man. Jesus saw a blind man from birth, and His disciples asked Him who had sinned, this man or his parents, to cause his blindness. *Jesus told them neither he nor his parents sinned, but it happened "so that the works of God might be displayed in him."*

He made mud with his saliva mixed with dirt, put it on the man's eyes and told him to go and wash in the Pool of Siloam. The man did as Jesus told him, and he went home—**seeing** everyone and everything in his path for the very first time.

What about our transgender children? Was their condition caused by our sin or theirs?

Or could it be that God will show His mighty works in them?

Psalm 116:1-2 (NIV)

I love the Lord, for he heard my voice;
He heard my cry for mercy.
Because He turned His ear to me,
I will call on Him as long as I live.

NOTE FROM THE AUTHOR:

If you would like more information about who I am and my mission statement, please go to www.susanbutlerlive.com.

Wishing you God's best as you continue your own journey.

Susan Butler
susan@susanbutlerlive.com
SusanButlerLive — Facebook page